"The role of the diversity professional is relatively new in the history of the legal services industry. In many attempts to introduce diversity, the effort has been an "add-on" activity for the organization. As the co-authors have demonstrated in their own organizations, however, diversity must be a part of the basic culture and structure of an organization for it to have significant impact. For diversity professionals and their management colleagues in such organizations, *Diversity in Action* will help them and their organizations achieve this more robust diverse culture that clients demand more and more from their service firms. *Diversity in Action* is essential reading not only for diversity professionals, but for other senior managers in law firms and other organizations."

David Van Zandt, President, The New School

"There's no clear career path to becoming a diversity professional within the legal profession. Diversity professionals come to their positions with uneven degrees of experience, training, and aptitude. Nevertheless, in those roles they often have significant amounts of responsibility without always having commensurate authority. This book fills a much-needed gap in supporting diversity professionals with practical information and workable strategies they can use to fulfill their own and their positions' potential."

Sandra Yamate, Chief Executive Officer, The Institute for Inclusion in the Legal Profession

"The benefits of working in, or doing business with, organizations that have an inclusive, diverse work environment are incalculable. Law firms and corporate legal departments have dramatically increased initiatives to create truly inclusive workplaces, where each individual is treated equitably and can thrive. However, we need only look, for example, to the percentage of Fortune 500 women CEOs (4.8% according to *Fortune*) or the percentage of African American attorneys in the U.S. (4.2% according to the *American Lawyer*) to realize that creating a diverse, inclusive work environment is no easy task. Even where minority groups show gains in actual numbers, the percentage that actually cross into partnership or upper management remains dismally small. Drawing on the depth and wealth of their impressive experiences, these authors have written the definitive guide for developing and sustaining successful diversity initiatives. Every professional involved in diversity work has been waiting for this easy to navigate, practical and inspirational manual. *Diversity in Action* is a must read text for diversity professionals at all levels as well as organization leaders who are grappling with how to get this right!"

Petal Modeste, J.D., MBA,
Assistant Dean and Dean of Career Services,
Columbia Law School

Diversity in Action

A Manual for Diversity Professionals in Law

Theresa D. Cropper
and Anna L. Brown

Cover Jill Tedhams/ABA Publishing.

Printed in the United States of America.

18 17 16 15 14 5 4 3 2 1

Library of Congress Cataloging-in-Publication Data

Cropper, Theresa, author.

Diversity in action : a manual for diversity professionals in law / Theresa Cropper, Anna L. Brown.

pages cm

Includes bibliographical references and index.

ISBN 978-1-61438-982-8 (alk. paper)

1. Diversity in the workplace--United States. 2. Law firms--United States--Personnel management. 3. Discrimination in employment--Law and legislation--United States. 4. Minority lawyers--Employment--United States. 5. Women lawyers--Employment--United States. I. Brown, Anna L., author. II. Title.

KF318.C76 2014

344.7301'133--dc23

2014032537

Discounts are available for books ordered in bulk. Special consideration is given to state bars, CLE programs, and other bar-related organizations. Inquire at Book Publishing, ABA Publishing, American Bar Association, 321 N. Clark Street, Chicago, Illinois 60654-7598.

www.ShopABA.org

ACKNOWLEDGMENTS

We are most grateful to our families, friends and colleagues for all of their support and encouragement in the writing of this book. In particular, we wish to thank our industry insiders for their wisdom, expertise and generous contributions. You have all inspired us to work harder, raise the bar higher and continue the quest for excellence in advancing diversity and inclusion in the legal profession and beyond. We would like to thank Perkins Coie and Shearman & Sterling for their support and efforts in this endeavor. We are ever optimistic that those of us on the front line of diversity will continue to advance these efforts.

Contents

INTRODUCTION

This manual is designed to assist those who are involved in diversity work. Although the primary focus is on diversity and inclusion initiatives in law firms and corporate legal departments, this book can be a useful tool for anyone who is pursuing activities or programs that are foundations of diversity work. Creating strategic alliances, developing strategies for short-term and long-term change, and creating, developing, and measuring programs and activities are important elements of this manual.

This guide can be used as a complete resource in its entirety or as a reference for certain areas. Whether you are planning a retreat or considering a supplier diversity program, this guide can offer advice and guidance and will provide a comprehensive approach toward a successful journey in developing change in an organization.

In general, diversity initiatives in the legal profession can be complex, as the ultimate goal is to change the behavior of the organization and weave this business practice, value, and philosophy into every aspect of how your firm or department does business—essentially, the fabric of the organization. The law industry is part of the foundation and matrix of society, and the introduction of a fundamental change can be a challenge—you should not expect that it will occur overnight, especially when existing practices have been profitable without fundamental changes in many years.

As the practice of law has become a cross-border and global business, including the introduction of real-time social media, there has been a sustained focus on diversity in the legal profession over the past ten years. The concept of diversity and inclusion is known to most, but its practice is still one that requires a careful plan so that it will mesh with the culture and business plan of each organization. This plan and practice must serve as the framework for the development and implementation of the organization's diversity and inclusion function. If a house does not have a solid foundation, it will not stand. This analogy holds true for workplace diversity and inclusion initiatives. The foundation or framework must be sound for the initiatives to be effective and impactful.

This manual is dedicated to sharing a detailed and user-friendly guide to establishing a comprehensive and functioning diversity and inclusion initiative in your organization. This is practical advice and guidance from diversity and inclusion practitioners (with a total of 75+ years of combined experience!), industry insiders and experts, and corporate leaders!

CHAPTER 1

STRATEGIC PLANNING

Or how to stop reacting to every idea and advances the mission proactively

Overview

Strategic thinking is essential in diversity work. The reality is that the demands on the diversity professional are such that the majority of the time can be spent simply responding and reacting to daily requests, regular reports, episodic opportunities, and unexpected concerns. The diversity professional who is not strategic runs the risk of reacting to what is presented, without creating proactive opportunities to manage the responsibilities of the position. An important skill is the ability to assess when and how to be strategic with key entities within the organization. This skill is crucial because it will empower the diversity professional to identify objectives and goals and ways to accomplish them in a specific time frame. The nature of the work and the position is such that it is easy to get lost and not understand the paths to success, or more basically, the definitions of success.

What Is Strategic and What Is Tactical?

A fundamental understanding of strategic thought and development means appreciating the difference between strategy and tactics. *Strategy* is the overall aim or goal of the efforts. *Tactics* are the smaller, less long-term, but significant steps needed to implement the strategy. Without strategic vision, important tactics can appear to be strategic, but will prove to be short-term. Consider the following example of strategy versus tactics.

Strategy versus Tactics

GOAL: Win the war

STRATEGY: Capture the town

TACTICS:

- Approach by sea. This entire effort can be divided into several important roles: assessment of country X's naval capability—what kinds of boats will be used, what kind of troops, timing, when and where, what support will be needed, who will lead, how equipment and weapons will be unloaded, etc.
- Capture the beach: Which place and why, who will lead, what kind of troops, what are the tactics for preparing to advance on the mountain, etc.
- Advance on the mountain and capture the fort: Who is the best to lead, what equipment is needed, what troops, when and how, etc.

The military example provides an easy visual to illustrate this distinction. The goal is to win the war with country X. An important strategy is to capture town Y, by the sea. The plans to land and capture the beach, the fort on the mountain by the beach, and the surrounding town are all tactical. As important and intricate as the plans to implement the goal of taking the town are, these plans are tactical. Therefore, if the plan is only to capture the beach, because it is in an important area, then there is no strategy as to why the beach is relevant to an overall strategy to win the war. Putting this analogy in the diversity context, many programs, events, and activities are tactical efforts. They should be part of larger, longer-term goals that have a greater influence toward effectuating real and tangible results in diversity.

The Diversity Planner

GOAL: Increase representation in ethnic demographics.

STRATEGY: Increase the number of ethnically diverse applicants from schools where students have been successful at your organization as well as five other key schools.

TACTICS:

- Create relationships with the law school's admissions, career, and student services offices.
- Make contact with the student organizations of those ethnicities in those schools; provide programming to those schools that will showcase the company or firm to students but also allow the firm to become aware of specific students in the pipeline.
- Create connections with the students early and often.

If there is a proposal to invest in schools that are not in those groups or that have never had a good representation in the law firm and company, then it is important to evaluate the decision within the context of the strategy. Understanding this difference is important when identifying what is strategic and what is tactical. Identifying a strategic goal allows the diversity professional to develop a route or journey to accomplish the goal, with the necessary timetable to identify exactly where one is on their journey.

Sometimes, it is difficult to be strategic. However, the diversity professional can be strategic on different levels, all of which are important. Whether creating a strategic plan for the organization, developing a strategy for the department or committee, or devising your personal strategic goals, there are some steps to employ. We will review some strategic approaches and methods to implement them.

Strategic Approach versus Strategic Plan

- A strategic approach means employing strategy to manage a situation.
- A strategic approach does not require the engagement of others and can be a work style or method used by the diversity professional.
- A strategic approach uses strategic thought to manage a situation within the control and confines of the professional.

EXAMPLE: The strategic plan is to increase demographics among ethnicities with a focus on specific schools where the yield and results have been positive.

A strategic approach is to understand the best and most successful ways to work with the schools. If one of your lawyers is influential in the school, use her "good offices" to approach the highest level of decision makers. If your company or firm is engaged in activity that may be beneficial to any of the schools (a community program, etc.), use that as a bridge to develop relationships. The strategic approach means being mindful of the impact analysis of each decision and how it will get you closer to your strategic goals. It is a careful and deliberate process that reflects thoughtful engagement, as if one were playing chess. The goal is to win the game; the strategic approach is to make the queen vulnerable. The queen is the increase in ethnic representation; working with the schools is a move by a knight, bishop, or rook. The game is to increase diversity representation.

Strategic Plan for the Organization

If the organization is committed to developing a strategic plan for diversity, that is the good news. Be careful what is wished for! Developing a strategic plan requires a strong investment of time, diligence, diplomacy, and compromise. To develop a strategic plan, one must appreciate the mechanics, the process, the diplomacy, and the diligence required, all while understanding the realities of the landscape of the organization. This appreciation and understanding must be filtered through tempered expectations that do not diminish optimism.

The development of a strategic plan is formulaic and applicable to most organizations and situations. It is the implementation of the formula that creates the unique tailor-made plan, like a recipe using ingredients that are indigenous only to the organization. The formula includes the identification of needs and goals, prioritizing them, assessing the challenges and opportunities, understanding the strengths and weaknesses, identifying realistic and pragmatic approaches and plans, and establishing a timetable.

When initiating a diversity strategic plan for the organization, it is important to establish, at the onset, that the fundamental goals of the diversity strategic plan are contained within any larger organizational strategic plan or annual strategies. *The diversity strategic plan cannot be a stand-alone goal that is not incorporated into or aligned with the overall strategy of the organization.* The goal for the strategic plan is a vision for the organization that defines the mission and specific goals and priorities of the diversity efforts and initiatives for the organization. This plan will also articulate how diversity goals are valued, prioritized, and incorporated into the organization.

Mechanics

- Create a strategic planning committee
- Engage key leaders
- Solicit input on needs, goals, and priorities
- Obtain good data and assessments
- Understand strengths, weaknesses, challenges, and opportunities
- Establish priorities
- Create a timeline with milestones

There is always strategy in strategy. Be strategic about selecting the members of your planning committee. Make sure there are heavy lifters on the committee, with a good balance of creative thinkers and results-oriented participants. Ensure that the usual suspects are included, but also include those who may represent differing opinions. Most important, this group should command respect on the issue of diversity as well as display leadership in the organization. They should have the capacity to make decisions and the internal relationships to get things done.

It is important to solicit effective ways to communicate and receive information. There are always differing styles of communication with differing groups, and considering these styles will yield better and more extensive information. Also, obtain as much quantitative data as necessary, for example, historical representation, attrition, retention, leadership demographics, committee representation, and any other quantifiable data that asks and answers questions that consistently arise. Find a way to present the information as concisely as possible. Decide the scope of the project and what is realistic. Establish a timetable with checkpoints for evaluation and review.

Process

- Have key leaders on the planning committee
- Make it easy for leaders to be engaged
- Identify key stakeholders and the best way to communicate with them
- Explore many methods of communications and input
- Exhibit transparency in the process and decisions
- Understand the challenges to consensus, majority decisions, and minority positions

It is critical that key organization leaders are involved in the process from the beginning and throughout the major milestones in development. The identification of needs, wishes, objectives, and goals requires opportunities to hear from as many stakeholders as possible. Engaging in assessments of needs and goals requires processes that allow all constituents to be heard. Being heard will become an important element when establishing priorities, as there are always many more needs and goals than can be managed by a strategic plan. It is also important to identify all stakeholders and the best method of communicating with each of those constituents. Allow enough time to acquire quality and quantifiable information. Depending on the scope of the plan, this could take months. Provide forums for input and provide as much transparency as possible on the identification of needs, goals, priorities, and methods. Solicit the organization's leaders' involvement in supportive and meaningful ways. Be sure that the strategic plan process and engagement is known to all those in the organization through formal and informal communication methods.

When sufficient information has been captured, it is important to devise ways to digest and present the information to the leadership of the strategic planning body. Establishing priorities and making decisions can require tremendous diplomacy as *the ultimate goal is to have a strategic plan that can be supported by all, with enthusiasm from the key diversity and organization leaders*. Whether operating by consensus, majority, or small-group decision makers, it is important to understand the impediments to decision making and the minority view. These understandings will factor into decisions regarding priorities and timetables. Be sure to filter all decisions through a reality check that considers time, resources, and support.

Strategic Plan for the Department or Diversity Committee

The diversity professional may function within a department, work directly with a diversity and inclusion committee, or both. These entities may or may not be firmly established and the relationships may or may not be clearly defined. Even so, a strategic plan can be developed for the department or the committee. The approach will be limited in scope and specific to the role and responsibility of the entity. Such a strategic plan requires an understanding of the entity or unit and its role, function, and status within the organization. The goal for this strategic plan is to provide definition and direction to the unit, defining success and timetables.

Mechanics

- Identify the primary role and responsibility of the unit
- Identify the potential roles and responsibilities of the unit
- Identify key strategic alliances
- Understand, assess, and review historical successes and challenges
- Assess the critical needs of the committee or department
- Communicate and quantify knowledge with data
- Assess the strengths
- Determine the resources
- Establish priorities
- Create a timeline with milestones and opportunities to assess and review

The mechanics of this strategic plan are usually limited to those who are directly involved or affected by the diversity department or committee. The assessment, including the "who are we and what do we do" phase, is an important beginning, as such questions alone can be the challenge and the solution to strategic planning for the unit. Once the challenges are explored thoroughly, then a review of the resources should include strategic alliances, as well as historical successes and goodwill. Gathering data, including honest feedback on the needs of the committee or department, will prove invaluable.

Enlisting objective or professional help in facilitating discussions and advancing the mechanics will facilitate more robust information and resolutions. It is important to communicate, collect data, assess, and review and determine needs, priorities, and timetables. Whether it is very basic and simplistic or more involved, for example with an outside consultant, this kind of exercise can prove invaluable in understanding the role of the diversity initiative within the organization.

Process

- Make it easy to be heard and to communicate
- Have transparency
- Be inclusive
- Be aware of challenges, opportunities, limitations, and successes
- Understand the challenges to decision making

Process is always important as it affects the quality of the results. The process is the methods used to implement a plan. In diversity work, it is crucial to always be inclusive in the process. Make note of the communications processes—how to include people, when to do so, and how groups are composed can become political considerations. The style of communication often dictates the perception and value of the project. It is important that the process for the diversity committee or department's strategic planning include as many members as possible. All voices should be heard because all workers will contribute to the overall effort.

An honest assessment of challenges and limitations is necessary to develop future planning. The planning process must employ a critical eye toward status, hierarchy, gravitas, political support, and alignment of the committee/department. Candid discussions about the pragmatic reality of the opportunities and challenges can yield a road map to developing priorities, short- and long-term. The process should include an understanding of the priorities and differing values of the different constituents. Developing a strategic plan for the committee or department will afford opportunities to brainstorm and problem share with individuals and alliances that will serve long-term partnerships. This process could and should yield the plan, but also make some inroads to creating relationships that can be strategic and mutually beneficial.

Pragmatic Tips for the Strategic Plan for the Department or Committee

- Determine the most urgent issues for the unit and what has been stated as the most important for both unit and firm
- Conduct a comparative analysis of the two
- Identity common elements and contradictory elements
- Identify five priorities
- Determine what it would take to accomplish them
- Rank the priorities by importance or rank them by pragmatic and realistic accomplishment
- Establish a timetable

Personal Strategy Plan

Sometimes it may be difficult to develop a diversity strategic plan for the organization, committee, or department. This does not preclude one from strategic planning in the role as the diversity professional. The diversity professional can always be strategic about what can be accomplished and how these accomplishments can be positioned strategically with other work. The diversity professional can, and should, determine what he or she can accomplish and be strategic about managing those accomplishments. The development and execution of this plan is solely dependent upon the diversity professional. The personal strategy plan is one that you have for your own role and performance as a leader of diversity within the organization. This plan is not necessarily for public consumption or review.

Mechanics

- Look at the job description
- Look at the 12-month and 6-month accomplishments
- List the greatest successes and reasons for them
- List unfinished business
- List big dreams
- Establish a five-year vision and a one-year vision
- Identify challenges and rank them
- Identify limitations
- Identify resources and alliances
- Identify what you think is most important and realistic and why
- Identify your long-term goals for you in this role
- Identify quick wins
- Identify specific challenges and how they will be managed
- Map a step-by-step strategy:
  - What is needed
  - Who is needed
  - How long is required (create a timetable)

The more strategic you are, the more control you will have over time, goals, and results. The day-to-day interruptions that occur will be viewed in context more quickly and priorities will be apparent. Decisions will be easier because they will either support and execute the strategic plan, or not. If not, then it should be clear why you should or should not invest any more time and resources.

To be less reactive requires a realistic plan for what can be accomplished. Whether the steps given in the "Mechanics" box are implemented with a more formal structured style or through mental exercises with limited notes and reminders, the mechanics of establishing a journey for the year, with a vision for the next five years, enables the diversity professional to assess his or her own effectiveness. The plan can be modest or formal, but it should yield a journey according to a strategy that is understood and valued. This becomes important when reacting to the day-to-day demands of the position. It helps you keep your footing in a job that never delivers a routine day.

Process

- Understand that this process requires self-awareness and self-assessment
- Be honest
- Avoid excuses
- With each priority identified, ask and answer five progressive "whys" on the relevance of that priority
- Understand your value proposition—what you bring to the table that advances the efforts
- Remind yourself why you accepted the position
- Evaluate your frustrations—why and when
- Consider the following:
  - How will this process contribute to your professional development goals?
  - What are your personal professional goals?
  - What are your needs, wants, and dreams?
  - What are your strengths?
  - What are your weaknesses?
  - What is your strategy to reconcile all of the above?

This process has elements of personal reflection in the context of professional accomplishments. Your honest self-assessment will contribute greatly to your success in diversity work. This is difficult work. Be kind to yourself as you explore your challenges and limitations. Understand what is beyond your control and what you can control. Be realistic about long-term visions. Big dreams can be broken into small steps or a few goals. It is not the grandiose, sweeping ideas that are usually part of this kind of personal strategic plan. Your personal and professional diversity journey will allow big dreams down a road of single goals and realistic plans.

What You Should Know

- Identify a few short-term and long-term goals.
- When deciding if you should adopt a new project or program or evaluating an existing one, ask yourself "why" five times.
    - Let's have an affinity group. Why? The identified group wants one. Why? They believe it will be helpful to the organization. Why? It will build community? Why is that helpful? It will form connections, provide education, and help with retention. Why is that helpful? If people are better informed, have relationships within the organization, and folks know how they are doing, it may be easier to anticipate situations that may affect departures.
- Always assess if what you are doing is bringing the organization closer to short-term or long-term goals.
- Understand why one is investing in a program, initiative, or policy.
- Evaluate your investments frequently. *It will not always be a direct and perfect correlation with goals, but if it builds community, a strategic alliance, or good will, it may be worth the time.*

CHAPTER 2

WHERE DOES THE BUCK STOP? ACCOUNTABILITY

Or how many constituents do you serve, actually

Overview

In many cases, the diversity effort is the newest department or team in the law firm or organization. This effort may also be an established part of the organization, but compared to other departments, such as human resources, recruitment, or marketing, diversity efforts usually became part of the organization after hierarchies are established. Where the core of this initiative resides can provide insight into the organization's perception and value of this effort. Who leads the effort, his or her title, and to whom he or she reports also reveal more information about the operation and function of diversity efforts within an organization.

Accountability

The diversity professional has inherent accountability within the organization for matters that impact the organization's diversity and inclusion commitment and goals. This accountability requires that critical information is communicated, valuable opinions are solicited, and essential support is obtained. Whether there is a direct or dotted line, connections between the diversity team and key departments and individuals should be facilitated by the diversity professional. Key entities and individuals have an informal accountability that should always be honored, regardless of the diversity team or department. For example, communication between the diversity team and the leaders of human resources and recruiting is essential. Further, it is important to establish and maintain connections with the chief administrative leader, members of senior leadership, and, of course, the diversity committee or counsel and diversity leaders.

Communication with the Highest Administrative Office

Whether it is with the chief operating officer, the management committee, the executive director, or an equivalent, it is necessary to establish a direct line of communication with the highest-level administrative office. Communication can be in the form of a quarterly status report or an annual review, but it should be concise, clear, and consistent. Proactively communicating directly with the administrative leader provides control over the messages conveyed. The diversity professional should take the lead to always control the message to the administrative office, including what is important, what is relevant, how resources are marshaled and distributed, and the relevant timetables. It is critical to also include successes that have been achieved and challenges to be managed. Regardless of the mode selected to communicate with this office, the method and frequency must be consistent. It is not advisable to have ad hoc, intermittent communication and updates because the goal is to provide reliable value-add information in a manner that conveys accountability and a need for regular reporting.

Communication with Firm and Department Leaders

As a best practice, the diversity professional or team should always have access to firm leaders, given the broad and often sensitive nature of the diversity function. If the structure does not allow for access, the diversity professional should still perceive his or her role as being accountable to senior leadership within the organization. The diversity professional should seek to provide senior leaders with value-add information and short updates on the firm's diversity efforts and successes. Senior level diversity professionals should interact regularly with senior management, and junior level professionals should find opportunities to interact with leaders, such as at recruiting events or diversity programs. Access to senior leadership is important and will assist in advancing the authenticity of the organization's commitment to diversity. Further, the time to establish a line of communication with senior management is not when a crisis arises, but throughout the year, so that management has a clear understanding and view of the organization's diversity and inclusion challenges, goals, and successes. It is no secret in understanding power within an organization that access to the decision makers is the basis of gravitas and clout.

Communication with the Diversity Committee or Council

Typically, the diversity committee or counsel is composed of professionals who have an interest in and/or responsibility for the organization's diversity efforts. Depending on the organization's structure, the diversity professional may report directly to this group. Whether the group is formal or informal, the diversity professional should establish a periodic as well as an informal method of communication with this group. Such communication allows for easy access to this important resource. Communication should include regular reports, but also informal updates with challenges and opportunities. Establishing this line of communication will set the tone and substance of any agendas to be developed.

Insight: A Closer Look at Accountability

Interview with Craig Courter, Law Firm Chief Operating Officer

Craig Courter, interviewed when he was Chief Operating Officer at Perkins Coie, now Global Chief Operating Officer at Baker & McKenzie, believes that the Chief Diversity Officer needs to have a seat at the table with the C-suite and the firm's Partner leadership. "Diversity can't be accomplished in a vacuum," Courter explained, "the CDO needs to partner with each Partner in Firm Leadership and the C-suite to set and drive the diversity agenda. While diversity can be categorized as a people function and classified into the Human Resources or Talent Management department, the person accountable for driving the diversity programs needs to have influence with the person leading practice groups—to address

Continued

Insight: A Closer Look at Accountability *Continued*

utilization and staffing; finances—to ensure reporting is proper and accurate; marketing—to help develop the firm's diversity brand, and business development—to ensure proper staffing on pitches and the fairness of other business development opportunities, to name a few."

"The CDO should be responsible for working with Partners and others to develop and to implement the Diversity strategy," Courter explained, "and the CDO need the authority to do that. Burying the CDO too deeply in the organization detracts from at least their apparent authority."

To achieve these goals Courter believes "the most important personal characteristic for a CDO is gravitas, Partners and others need to recognize the CDO as an expert in the field and a person of substance and depth of personality." Courter identifies three more specific characteristics when asked what skills he thought were necessary in managing these kinds of relationships, "I'll lay out a few things. The first is you've got to know your stuff. You've got to know the area. You've got to know the key people from the other firms. You've got to know the companies at the forefront of driving outside law firms to become more diverse. You've got to know what people do to promote diversity. And, you've got to be seen in the legal industry as a thought leader. I think the second thing is listening. Organizations are different and a new CDO needs to do a lot of listening to put things in perspective. I think listening is really key when you're working with practice groups, or affinity groups and the like. They want your ideas, but they're struggling to say something as well, and you really need to figure out where they are trying to articulate and put it in terms of diversity best practices. And how can you do that? You've got to listen—actively listen—to ferret that out. Also, the CDO deals with emotional issues and needs to listen closely on points raised to fully understand them before responding or taking action. I think the third is organization and getting things done."

Courter continues: "Inside the organization a good CDO will know the diverse lawyers and staff and takes the time to understand their special strengths and challenges. This takes traveling to the offices and various meetings to build and foster these relationships. A good CDO will be able to speak frankly with someone who is underperforming, and having a trusted relationship up front can make that easier and more effective, and will be able to speak frankly with firm leadership when a diverse lawyer or staff is not getting proper development. These discussions require prior trust building."

Courter believes that accountability in relationships is only as important as the trust, which he defines as critical. "I think the biggest issue here is trust. I think that to be a diversity professional, you have to establish and keep establishing trust from the diverse teammates and the people who are leading various areas of the firm. If they have a conversation with you and they said something incorrectly or they're struggling to understand a concept or they were just on the wrong side of the issue and you helped them see the right side, then nobody's going to ever hear of that. That's the trust you need, you need to be a confidential source of counseling and the like, and that is really important. You need to build a safe environment for people to talk about diversity and make mistakes, or at least refine their position, as they do and not be reminded about it later."

Courter identifies the following elements as critical in establishing accountability and strong relationships with key decision makers in the organization: regular and systematic reporting of a strategy, business plan, and data, and the status of that strategy and plan; strong relationships with key leaders of practice groups or business groups, offices, and affinity groups, born out of regular visits and communication; the creation of a safe environment for trusted communications that is designed around honest sharing of ideas and educational development in diversity; and the diversity professional must be a senior leader who is a thought leader and employs strategic and tactical solutions through listening and understanding key stakeholders.

What You Should Know

- Ask yourself who the stakeholders are in every project, initiative, or strategy. Who is directly affected or who has a direct impact on the execution of this effort?
- Keep your stakeholders informed on a regular basis through formal reports and casual conversations. Remember that "Hey, I was just touching base to keep you in the loop" call can go a long way.
- Try to make information and progress reports easily available on a regular basis.

CHAPTER 3

FINDING THE OPPORTUNITY AND TAKING CHARGE

Or how to effectively step in

Overview

There will always be opportunities to intersect an organization's diversity and inclusion efforts and goals with existing systems, functions, and events. As you employ strategy in your diversity efforts, remember to step back and think through the opportunities, challenges, resources, alliances, goals, priorities, and timetables. Remembering to understand varying definitions of successful outcomes by different stakeholders will assist you in becoming strategic in approaches to events and opportunities that occur occasionally or regularly.

Episodic Opportunities

As events or difficulties arise, the diversity professional should always be prepared to be strategic, evaluating and strategizing to determine how these events or opportunities can be converted into contributions to the long-term diversity efforts and goals. Aside from episodic opportunities, there are regular events that should be considered in diversity strategy. If there are regular meetings, retreats, conferences, or events, consider whether these regular occurrences can provide opportunities to advance diversity efforts. Utilizing existing systems to further diversity and inclusion goals is necessary.

OPPORTUNITY AND CRISIS MANAGEMENT

When something happens that gains the unexpected attention of the organization or department's leaders, immediately determine whether there is an opportunity for diversity management. Most diversity-related crisis management leads to an appreciation of the diversity professional and heightened attention on diversity. Consider a group lateral hire or departure—either provides an opportunity to be strategic. Employ the methods discussed, but focus on the following:

- What is the impact analysis for diversity?
- What are the challenges?
- What are the opportunities?
- What can be learned?
- What are the long-term goals?
- What are the immediate concerns or issues?
- What are the necessary and immediate next steps?
- What is the timetable?
- What role does the diversity professional play?

ENGAGEMENT AT REGULAR MEETINGS

Every organization has regular meetings. These could be organized by specific function or hierarchal level. They could be gatherings of the organization's leaders or groups. Perhaps the practice groups are meeting or the practice group leaders are meeting. Whatever the arrangement in your organization, you should examine these meetings strategically to determine how they can add value to the diversity goals and efforts. Consider the following when examining these meetings strategically:

- What is the intersection of organizational diversity goals and this meeting?
- What strategic alliances exist between the diversity goals and this meeting?
- What are the outcomes of this meeting?
- What are the advantages of the audience?
- What are the shared concerns, values, and needs?
- What are the mutual benefits?
- What does the diversity team need from this group?

- What is the strategic communication with this group?
- What is a realistic ask? What is needed to get the ask?
- How do you make the ask?
- How is success measured?
- Is there an opportunity for a long-term structured relationship?
- Can mutual goals be subsumed into overall goals? How does that happen?
- Who is the liaison within the group?
- Can encounters be regularized?

Recurring Events

Retreats and conferences provide great targeted opportunities to be strategic in your diversity efforts and goals. Because conferences and retreats are usually subject-specific, look for the alignment of programs with your diversity goals. Recurring events can be occasions such as an anniversary or annual remembrance or celebration. Always ask: What are the intersections, alliances, mutual concerns, needs, and benefits? What are the advantages of the group and what is the greatest need of the group? You may have a opportunity to communicate a message or educate a group.

What You Should Know

THINK ABOUT IT:

- There is always an opportunity to learn, teach, and grow.
- Listen first.
- Ask yourself what is expected of the diversity professional. Are you competent to do that job or do you need outside professional expertise?
- Define success and then understand what it will take to achieve it.
- What is a win? Are there levels of winning? Define them along the way. *Never devalue a win, no matter how small.*

CHAPTER 4

STRUCTURE, BUDGET, AND BRAND

Or how are you going to do this? With whom? And how will you present to your internal and external audiences?

Overview

There are many considerations when examining and developing the administrative aspects and structure of diversity and inclusion initiatives in an organization. The organization and the diversity professional must consider and appreciate where the responsibility for administering the organization's diversity initiative resides and its impact, as well as the fundamental administrative responsibilities, which can vary widely from organization to organization; however, there are common principles and formats that should be considered, regardless of structure. As this may be a new position in the firm or company, there is often an examination of where the diversity function should reside, and the seniority level at which the administrative lead is best placed in your organization. In this section, we will discuss:

- Structure
- Budgeting
- Branding

The diversity professional's title will vary among organizations and depend on the level of seniority and experience. Titles range from the junior level, such as administrator, specialist, and coordinator, to the more senior, such as manager, director, counsel, or chief diversity officer. In addition to the title determination, diversity professionals must appreciate the scope of the position, the department where the diversity function resides, and to whom he or she is accountable administratively, structurally, and politically. Before a basic analysis of possible titles, contemplate the following questions to appreciate the context and position of the diversity professional. One must consider how the diversity position is perceived and the level of responsibility or gravitas allowed by the seniority, placement, and accountability contained in the position.

Determine the following within your organization:

- Is there a diversity department or a reasonable facsimile thereof?
- Who is the administrative leader of such a department or group?
- Is the diversity professional responsible for strategic planning or recommendations for strategic planning?
- Does the diversity professional have budget responsibility and signature authority? Who develops the budget? Who approves the budget?
- Who are the firm or company equivalents to the diversity professional?
- Are there clearly stated roles and responsibilities for the diversity professional? Oftentimes, this position evolves organically and a job description did not precede the professional.
- What is the organizational structure and what are the formal lines of communication between the diversity professional and other professionals and departments?

Before discussing titles, it is worth mentioning that such titles and job descriptions can and will vary widely among firms and companies or law departments. It is also important to note that having a diversity administrator or coordinator at the law department level, with a chief diversity officer who has corporation-wide responsibility, is a common structure in corporate law. These title definitions also represent common practices and often there may be multiple diversity professionals working together. A manager may have an administrator or a director may have a manager or coordinator working with him or her.

STRUCTURE

Diversity Titles

Consider the following titles and related levels of seniority, responsibility, and accountability.

Administrator or coordinator: This position is typically junior and intended to support a senior person who has more frontline responsibility for implementing and executing the organization's diversity initiatives. The diversity professional in this position may be the primary point of contact for all programs, events, and administrative matters. This person may work directly with a manager or director who provides administrative, programmatic, and strategic oversight.

Manager: A diversity manager is a supportive midlevel position whose primary responsibility is to implement and execute the organization's diversity strategy and programming; the position typically does not require the diversity professional to research and develop the organization's strategic plan. The diversity manager usually reports to the person who has the budget and programming responsibility and authority, such as the director or chief diversity officer. In some cases, this person works alone as the sole leader of the diversity efforts.

Director: A diversity professional at the director level is part of senior management. He or she has budget responsibility (and may also have budget authority) and programmatic authority and responsibility, and is charged with strategic consultation with senior leadership and developing and implementing the organization's strategic plan. There is usually a support staff person who is dedicated to working with the person in the director position.

Diversity counsel or special counsel: This position is usually occupied by a law firm partner or senior level attorney who spends part of his or her time dedicated to working on diversity matters within the organization. Typically, there is a reduced billable hour requirement and compensation is negotiated for the diversity role and reduced law practice responsibility. This position is at the strategic level, with dedicated administrative support, such as a diversity administrator or coordinator.

Chief diversity officer: This position is at the highest management level and reports directly to the senior management of the organization, such as the managing partner, chief operating officer, or chief executive officer. This position usually requires involvement in firm policy, strategy, and execution. This position typically has another position who will be a direct report to the CDO. Responsibilities include budget management and programmatic decision-making authority.

Diversity Department/Function

To start, consider the scope of the organization's diversity efforts. What is the range of operation or authority of the diversity professional within the organization? It is helpful and often necessary to conduct a candid internal assessment to ensure the success of the role of the diversity professional. Whether this assessment is formal or informal, an honest discussion with key decision makers or in the interviewing process is vital to understanding the expectations and possible limitations of the diversity efforts within the organization, as this will determine the expectations and limitations of the diversity professional's position.

Important Questions to Ask When Understanding the Diversity Function

Level of Responsibility: Does this position have primarily administrative functions? Is the diversity professional expected to complete surveys, repeat the execution of existing programs, and respond to correspondence regarding sponsorship and recruitment? Is this position on the "front line of diversity" where key decision makers will give directives or refer matters to this person for one or two-step resolutions? For example, is this where surveys are sent for data insertion? Does this person have budget authority and the ability to make key decisions regarding resources?

Level of Seniority: Does this position have any strategic functions? Is this person included in the executive level discussions on the identification of challenges and solutions? Is this person included in hiring, promotion, compensation and termination discussions and decisions? Is this person regularly included in many or most of the high level and strategic firm/law department discussion? Does this person regularly consult with firm leaders-managing partners, practice group leaders, key committee chairs?

Level of Accountability: Is the diversity position tactical? Is this person identified to manage solutions already created? Does strategic information filter down to this position and this person is expected only to implement identified solutions? Is this a person who may be identified for membership on temporary committees that strategic committees have designated for specific implementation on key issues? Will this person be a member of a task force on retention, whose tasks are to find solutions within the directives identified by the strategic groups? Does the position manage solutions already identified?

As stated in Chapter 2 on accountability, advancing diversity and inclusion within an organization is in every department's purview and is every department's responsibility. Diversity directives will impact every department at some level. In some cases historically, the diversity function has been an additional administrative burden to some departments and when a diversity professional joins the firm, company, or department, there is a tendency to convert all functions, responsibilities, and connections to that new person or department. This is not an effective response to integrating the diversity professional or the goals of the organization's diversity initiatives. While the diversity professional may have responsibility for some of those functions, it is important to integrate and include the organization's diversity goals in many strategic and tactical functions. Some of the responsibilities of the diversity professional may be obvious and some areas may have shared functions and overlap. Examining the fundamental aspects of the administrative purview by responsibility may facilitate the understanding and cooperation that must exist between all departments to achieve the diversity needs of the organization.

RESPONSIBILITIES

There are several organizational areas and activities that the diversity professional should claim ownership of, including: the measurement of diversity data; directing diversity committees and diversity support networks; ensuring that diversity issues are discussed at firm-wide programs and retreats; sponsorships with third-party organizations; and budgeting for diversity programs.

Data Management

Diversity professionals should be intricately and intimately involved with diversity data management. This includes the identification of methodologies, categories, and distribution. Data is critical and integral to managing and evaluating diversity initiatives. Often this information is considered sensitive and must be handled with integrity. Those who handle, collect, and distribute diversity data must have a clear understanding of what is contained in the data and the particular idiosyncrasies that exist in your organization. One must consider: How it is collected? Who is included in those collections? How is this information categorized? This is important information that needs input and direction from the diversity professional. For an in-depth discussion regarding data management, see Chapter 14 on metrics.

An important aspect of data management is methodology. It is critical to determine the method by which diversity data and information will be collected. This discussion may include consideration of software opportunities; how and when to integrate data from multiple databases (such as finance and human resources); when and where to distinguish between head count and full time equivalent (FTE); the scope of data collection (such as including persons, offices, or operations outside of the United States); or quantifying attrition, retention, and departures. It is vital for the diversity professional to be included in this discussion and to add perspective on the impact analysis of these methodologies. For example, would an FTE count produce different numbers than a head count? Does the organization collect data for attrition differently than for retention? Does the organization collect data on veterans, openly LGBT persons, or persons with disabilities? Does historical data offer the information needed for a year-to-year analysis? Is the data static or does it change permanently when new data is entered?

Categories (race, ethnicity, gender, LGBT, disability, year employed, FTE, veterans) are important, particularly when considering data collection for external requests and for internal diversity and inclusion analysis. It also may be important with respect to affinity group or inclusion network identification, depending on your organization's structure and policies with respect to such groups (this is discussed more fully in Chapter 10 on affinity groups). There may be policy questions that emerge when considering firm or company titles. Further, there may be important distinctions for groupings of categories and how and when such groupings should be used, for example, when collecting U.S. data, some specific ethnic categories that may not be captured separately by standard Equal Employment Opportunity Commission (EEOC) classifications. Consider that persons of Middle Eastern descent are classified as white by the EEOC. The organization may wish to acknowledge its ethnic identity. How does the organization identify affinity groups/inclusion networks, and does it match your categories? Is there a South Asian affinity group/inclusion network? How will the organization capture the category of two or more races? Will one of the races be counted in form categorizations? (Some two or more races members want to also be identified as of one group, but one cannot double count them in public reporting. The organization may identify them internally for affinity group or other purposes. For example, someone who is two or more races and identifies as an African American, but they are biracial, can be a member of that Affinity group and the diversity professional can explain his/her numbers in recruiting efforts. Are there titles and categories for employees who are not a targeted group of your diversity efforts, such as contract lawyers, conflicts lawyers, patent agents, and so on?

Distribution of data is highly sensitive and requires strategic consideration. Who gets what data, when, and how? Who vets this data before it is distributed? Who knows which data is based on head count versus FTE and whether those categories are consistently reported, providing education on the distinctions between the two when there is confusion? Who keeps certain lists that may be offline, such as LGBT data that is public for collective counting purposes, but private for any data that could provide personal identification? What information is public and what information should be public?

The answers to these questions reside with the diversity professional, who must work from a proactive perspective regarding the data. The diversity professional must know which external publications use head count verses FTE, or whether the affinity groups need special identification. The diversity professional must also understand the intricate aspects of data management to ensure that information reported is accurate and has integrity and that the data collected captures what is necessary for current and strategic purposes. Until these data management questions are explored collectively between the diversity team and data management departments, the response to requests will be reactive rather than proactive. The diversity professional must guide the strategic collection of data that will allow the organization to study real-time and historical data responses to important questions on recruitment, retention, and promotion. To do so, it is essential that the diversity professional is central to the data management of the firm. Please see Chapter 14 for an in-depth discussion on metrics.

Surveys

Law firms, corporate legal departments, and other legal organizations receive many requests for diversity data. Requests may come from publications, bar associations, clients, and other nonprofit organizations. The organization should develop a work distribution of deliverables required by each survey request. Usually, a mix of data and narrative is required. Often, data is needed from more than one department or area. In other instances, multiple departments may need to supply narrative information. When a narrative is required, the response should include input, if not direction, from the diversity professional. In many instances, a prepared template developed by the diversity professional that generally describes the organization's diversity and inclusion efforts should be used as a starting point for all narrative discussions. Such templates are prepared in advance by the diversity professional or team and include input from several internal areas and departments, including the organization's marketing department.

The responsibility for the particular survey may rest with a specific department and/or attorney, or it may rest solely with the diversity professional or department. In all instances, however, the diversity professional must always be aware of the survey and involved in its final distribution. The diversity professional should review the final copy to ensure that it is consistent with, and conforms to, the methods used to respond to other diversity surveys and to assess if there are any concerns with the data reporting. Keep in mind there is also a need to coordinate the time management of surveys. Surveys may be quarterly, annually, or appear unexpectedly and episodically. Thoughtful and appropriate responses require time, and the diversity professional is usually a department of one or two. The diversity professional can be helpful in the creation of a methodology for the timetable for the completing the survey.

Diversity Committee and Affinity Group/ Inclusion Network Support

The diversity professional has a key role in the support, development, and management of the diversity committees and/or affinity groups or inclusion networks. Whether the diversity committees or subcommittees are firm- or department-wide or are in specific offices, the diversity professional serves an integral role in managing and supporting the groups and in many instances also in developing them. If such groups and the management thereof do not already exist, then certainly the diversity professional must consider their creation to be part of developing the organization's strategic plan. In the interim, however, the functions of many of these groups will reside with the diversity professional. These committees and/or groups should be organized with regular meetings, agendas, programs, initiatives, and a review process. Most importantly, they should have a strategic plan with stated goals and metrics. The diversity professional must support, provide guidance to, and encourage leadership within the group with respect to establishing agendas and executing activities and programs. The diversity professional must meet with the committee leaders or chairs to establish and advance the agenda. The diversity professional should encourage leadership within the group and can assist in the creation and development of the programs, ensuring that group initiatives are consistent with the goals and plans of the overall diversity efforts. The diversity professional can also work with the groups to assist them in determining when and how they will measure their success. Please see Chapter 10 for additional discussion on affinity groups.

Programs

Arguably one of the most important platforms for advancing your organization's diversity goals will be programs and initiatives. Such programs and initiatives should be developed around themes of retention, inclusion, advancement, recruitment, and community building. Whether or not the diversity professional is taking the lead to develop the strategies or concepts for these programs, he or she must be involved in their implementation and execution. The diversity professional can be instrumental in determining the most effective methods for the success of a particular program. Whether through the identification of potential speakers, suggestions for particular venues, checking for conflicts or concerns on dates, or defining methods of outreach and communications about the event or program, the diversity professional role is focused on advancing the overall objectives of the organization and adds value as it builds bridges to departments, communities, and groups of people. For additional discussion on programs, please see Chapter 11.

Retreats

A growing number of law firms and legal departments have retreats centered around diversity and the promotion of a more inclusive work environment. More and more organizations consider it an important part of their programming to advance diversity and inclusion goals. The diversity professional has a key leadership role in the development and planning of all such retreats. First, he or she works with group leaders to develop the strategic goals and objectives of the retreat, including the theme, agenda, and structure, and ensures it fits with the overall diversity goals of the organization. Further, the diversity professional should participate in meetings with planners and consultants to select the venue, date, and schedule. The diversity professional should be responsible for the management of the retreat in all aspects, from the administrative details and agenda development to the completion of a final report. See Chapter 13 for an in-depth discussion on retreats.

Sponsorships

Many nonprofit and advocacy groups, such as student organizations, bar associations, and community organizations, rely on the financial and in-kind support of law departments and law firms. In certain instances, the diversity professional must manage these relationships through direct involvement with his or her committee leadership and active participation in the organization's activities. Typically, the diversity professional provides advice, counsel, and sometimes analysis of the who and why of recommended sponsorships. In addition to the relationship represented in the sponsorship, there is usually an accompanying program or event that requires management. The diversity professional should work with the organization's marketing professionals to coordinate advertisement creation and language. These decisions and relationships may also be managed in coordination with the organization's affinity group/inclusion network leadership. Further, the diversity professional should work with the affinity group/inclusion network leadership, if relevant, to coordinate attendance at the sponsored event and the evolution of the relationship between the organizations. The diversity professional should be a primary point of contact and should have the ability to articulate the value of the sponsorship.

Budgeting

At the senior level, the diversity professional will typically have budgetary responsibility. This would include the development, maintenance, management, and reconciliation of budgetary expenditures as defined by the department or firm.

The organization's diversity budget and the specific line items contained therein will vary from one organization to another and may be complicated. The budget should, however, reflect the structure and purview of the department or team. Beyond listing the line items, there should be some policy considerations when determining what is in the diversity budget and why. These policies should explore the standard by which an expense is deemed to be a diversity team expense. Questions that may be asked to determine whether the item or expense is specific to the diversity efforts or if it serves a function for a diverse population include the following:

- Is sponsoring a school that is in an African American neighborhood a diversity expense, or perhaps an expense of the black lawyers' affinity group, or a charitable contribution expense?
- Is supporting a pipeline program designed to attract students to law, which includes visits and interaction with the students, a diversity expense or a community service expense?
- If there is a goal of supporting pipeline programs, does that change the decision?
- Should the Hispanic job fair be a diversity budget expense or a recruiting expense?
- Would a coach for an Asian attorney be a diversity expense or a professional development expense?

The answers to these questions are in the organization's policies. When exploring and developing these policies, start with a review of all firm policies. If coaches are provided for attorneys, remember that just because an attorney is a member of an ethnic minority group does not mean the cost should come from a different budget. If one diversity goal is to develop a pipeline, then perhaps a high school pipeline project in an underserved community is a diversity expense. If recruitment pays for job fairs, and it is an overall firm goal to include diversity in recruiting, then the Hispanic job fair is a recruitment expense. If the Latino affinity group wants to connect with the students after the job fair, that is a diversity expense.

Potential Line Items in the Diversity Budget

Expenses

- Training and professional development for staff
- Travel
- Sponsorships
- Diversity hiring (scholarships, etc.)
- Diversity programming (seminars, retreats, etc.)
- Affinity group/inclusion networks
- Diversity committee and affinity group meetings and programming
- Diversity awareness education and training
- Membership in ethnic bar associations
- Publications (marketing materials, etc.)
- Professional development and leadership training for diversity leaders
- Consultants, resources, and memberships
- Entertainment
- Departmental supplies, incidentals, etc.

In addition to developing the budget, it is critical for the diversity professional to ensure that expenses stay within budgetary limits. Leaders of the diversity committee and affinity groups/inclusion networks must be challenged to stay within predetermined budgets in connection with programs, initiatives, retreats, and so on. Monthly and quarterly budget reports should be established to track diversity spending, verify the accuracy of expenses, and make an effort to avoid overages.

BRANDING

A brand identity is a strategic means to identify, promote, and advance the organization's diversity and inclusion goals, internally and externally. The brand associates the organization's commitment through images and/or words with the organization's diversity efforts internally and externally. The diversity brand should be developed with the organization's marketing department and must be consistent and compatible with the organization's overall brand identity. It is critical to include key decision makers in the development of a brand identity. The brand should consistently carry and present the organization's message and commitment to diversity and inclusion.

The process of developing the brand should include the creation of a small working group, an assessment from the internal community on what the brand should represent, and the identification of the images and language that will be reflected in the brand. This process requires an effective working relationship with the organization's internal marketing professionals, who will probably be assigned the task of developing the brand. Once an identity has been established, it is the responsibility of the diversity department, team, or professional to assure that the brand is used consistently. One way to accomplish this is through the formation of templates when developing the brand identity. Templates should be developed for ads, HTML, invitations, newsletters, banners, stationery, PowerPoints, and signs, and also used consistently in affinity group notices, activities, presentations, announcements, and other forms of communication. The development of all diversity materials can have a beginning point with the template.

The diversity professional should encourage all departments of the organization to utilize the diversity brand in connection with diversity-related initiatives and to promote the advancement of diversity and inclusion both in and outside of the organization. Consistent use of the brand identity serves to educate the internal and external community, while providing a visual that immediately identifies the organization with the goals of its diversity and inclusion efforts. Please see Chapter 5 for an additional discussion on marketing and communications.

Communication between the Client and Law Firm

One of the many responsibilities of diversity professionals in law firms and legal departments is communication between the client and the law firm. Oftentimes, the communication is through formal, yet very traditional means—the bill and/or the diversity survey. The *diversity survey* can be a report that is monthly, quarterly, annual, or biannual. The information requested can range from basic demographic data to specific information on retention or billing demographics. Sometimes these requests require a basic level of reporting, and sometimes they require sophisticated projections and analysis. The client receives and manages the information in many ways. The range of possible responses from the client include acknowledging the survey; analyzing it with feedback; requiring meetings; and/or consequences such as awards, financial incentives, and more or less work from the client.

One of the more sophisticated client surveys and communications is the Microsoft Law Firm Diversity Program. This survey requires regular reporting and monitoring of specific data. Known as a consistent and dedicated actor in the legal diversity field, Microsoft is one of the best examples of effective diversity partnership and communications between company and law firm. Their Law Firm Diversity Program incentivizes law firms to increase diversity in their firm or in the numbers of diverse lawyers working on Microsoft matters. In addition, their legal department, under the leadership of their general counsel, Brad Smith, meets annually with outside counsel to discuss the diversity program as well as opportunities to partner on specific diversity programs. What is most impressive about Microsoft's effort is the team effort of diversity volunteers from their legal department. Their many efforts, including the Diversity IP Summit for law students, a mentoring program, attendance and support of many affinity bar conventions, and various pipeline programs, are all spearheaded and staffed by members of the legal team. Oftentimes these efforts are leadership development opportunities for the volunteers.

One of the leaders of this effort is Mary Snapp, Vice President and Deputy General Counsel of Microsoft. With ten years of diversity work in the legal department, Snapp is former chair of the diversity committee and now executive sponsor of diversity efforts. She currently co-chairs the diversity team, a group of 70 to 75 volunteers who support a broad range of diversity efforts. These volunteers support four committees whose chairs are accountable to Snapp for delivering on their goals. In addition, this team is also supported by a full-time diversity and inclusion program manager, who works on the legal department diversity initiatives while housed in the human resources group.

Insight: From an Industry Expert

Interview with Mary Snapp, Vice President and Deputy General Counsel, Microsoft

Microsoft is one of the few legal departments with dedicated full-time diversity professionals. Aligned with the global corporate diversity structure, the legal department diversity manager specifically focuses on the efforts of the legal department. "Our diversity team within the legal department started to grow and scale up. It became clear that we needed to have help to manage the logistics of program management. The person had to be able to manage our relationships with the various outside affinity groups, they had to manage the volunteer groups, and they had to create the dashboard where we measured our success. At the same time, our corporate Microsoft Global Diversity and Inclusion group also began to grow, increase resources and identify diversity program professionals within the human resources department. So we hired the first diversity professional in the legal group five or six years ago. He reports to HR and that enables him to align with the broad corporate strategy, which really is global diversity and inclusion with employees based in 50 countries."

The diversity manager serves as a quasi "executive director" to the committees, sponsors, and key stakeholders of the many diversity programs and activities in the legal department. Snapp describes many of the roles and responsibilities of the manager: "a very strategic resource, intimately involved in the decisions and directions of the programs, sets the agenda," and "stays up with research and literature." In very close working relationships with the diversity leadership, the diversity professional manages regular work. "We have quarterly meetings which are check-ins against our dashboard. We set our budget, and we plan for the next quarter. We plan our communications, what internal communications we're going to send and what outcomes we want from them. We are always looking for great talent."

Very similar to its law firm counterpart, Microsoft's diversity professional's responsibilities include strategic development, recruiting, retention, program development, research and analysis, and execution of the department's initiatives. There is a strong connection and communication between the Microsoft diversity manager and the diversity professionals of the law firms that provide services to Microsoft. There are many opportunities for the diversity leaders to intersect on mutual activities and efforts and Microsoft drives that effort and communication through its manager and volunteers. Whether it is mutual support of pipeline programs, support of each other's diversity efforts or attending functions together, Microsoft works closely with the diversity professionals in the law firms. With ten years of experience, Snapp offers some sage advice to diversity professionals in law firms: "I think it's very important for the diversity professional to think about in some ways as you might think about running a business. You need to have resources, to have people who are willing to work with you, to have a set of accountabilities, and to have a budget and you need to have check-ins. I think it's really important for a diversity professional to network and to stay connected to trends in the profession and to continue to both generate and to get great ideas from other people. And the diversity professional also needs to work to develop programs internally that help to ensure that you can retain the great people that you attract."

Snapp's advice: "I would say for someone who is thinking about these programs, don't be overwhelmed, just start. It's like the first day of your life when you decide you're going to exercise and you know that once you

Continued

Insight: From an Industry Expert *Continued*

get going you will be enthusiastic and thrilled to do it, and you just need to get started. You just need to go."

Microsoft Law Firm Diversity Program Partners with Law Firms

There are many kinds of surveys and communications between law firm and client. One of the most interesting is Microsoft's Law Firm Diversity Program. This is a program that offers law firms an option to increase their fee through compliance with diversity metrics chosen by the firm. "We started in 2008. We work with our largest providers of outside counsel and we offer a bonus of two percent of the fees for the year to that law firm. We provide a program for them where we set goals with them to either increase the diverse demographics of the firm or to increase the number of diverse lawyers working on our matters. We started out focused on racial and ethnic minorities and women, and over time, we've expanded the scope of the program as well, to include support for veterans, for people with disabilities, and also for openly LGBT persons as well. We also tied the success of the program to our own senior leadership team in the legal department. We set a goal that if less than 75 percent of the law firms in the program reached their goals, we would dock our own cash bonuses for the year in order to provide some accountability.

The program is a different kind of survey. It requires law firm quarterly monitoring to ensure that the annual numbers are compliant. It also requires a close relationship between the law firm and client. Microsoft and the law firm need to check in regularly. "That very first year we didn't reach the goals. The firms didn't reach the goals and we ended up contributing the (bonus) money to a program to increase diversity in the profession from college to law school, but we learned that we needed to partner much more closely with our law firms and we needed to be committed together for success. So we revised the program so that we reported more easily and more quickly; we beefed up the mentoring program that existed with our law firms. We have found that law firms are meeting the goals of the program more frequently by increasing diverse lawyers on our matters than more broad increase in the representation of the firm."

Microsoft continues to tweak the Law Firm Diversity Program. Its success is predicated on a close working relationship between law firms and Microsoft. Microsoft assigned key diversity leaders to the law firms, and there are numerous ways to support the success of the program. These efforts include CLE programs at Microsoft by law firm attorneys, joint sponsorship of mentoring programs between law firm associates and Microsoft lawyers, and many activities that allow the lawyers to better know each other, their needs, and their abilities.

Microsoft's Legal Department as a Model for Driving Diversity and Leadership

A strong component of the diversity initiatives at Microsoft is the large number of volunteers who work on the various diversity programs. "We say that they are volunteers in that most of the time they have raised their hand to tell us they want to participate in this very important effort. We ensure that their manager knows of their interest, when they write their performance reviews and that they've set a goal for their participation as part of their annual performance reviews."

Volunteerism at Microsoft is also leadership development. Volunteering for diversity provides exposure and skills development, such as speaking and program management. Snapp explains, "The people who volunteer for our diversity group have several opportunities. They get a lot of visibility with our executive leadership in terms of presenting. They have an ability to do external outreach in terms of speaking. They bring back information from outside, which is very important, so that we don't get isolated, and we recognize them in very visible ways over the course of the year. It is a great career development opportunity [and] it turns out to be a great retention tool for our really high-potential people. It is absolutely a critical part of the fabric of our department." Microsoft recognizes their volunteers at all hands meetings, where thousands of people listen to diversity presentations and recognitions. There are also quarterly meetings with the executive sponsors and the general counsel, where volunteers have opportunities to get visibility.

What You Should Know

- Understand the political reality of diversity within the organization. The structure and budget will give you some insight. Then be realistic about your goals within this political context. Make sure you have the staff and resources to execute any plans you may want to present.
- Be creative and collective with budget. There are many ways to share your resources and find ways to co-sponsor activities and efforts that will advance more than one department. Look for symmetry with other departments that naturally intersect or are interdependent upon diversity.
- Be efficient and effective with your monies. Understand the value received and always quantify the value of an economic investment. Was that sponsorship worth it? Did it meet your goals and expectations?
- If you choose a brand identity for diversity, use it often and with consistency. Develop protocols for the use of the logo. Insure that it is branded on all materials. Make sure that all the different entities, affinity groups, marketing, appreciate the protocols and enforce them.

CHAPTER 5

COMMUNICATIONS FOR THE DIVERSITY PROFESSIONAL

Or how, when and to whom to get your message

Overview

Providing clear and concise communication with respect to your institution's diversity strategies and programs is essential. In any diversity program, there will be a need to inform, educate, promote, and/or persuade. The tools used to communicate across these needs must be effective. Communication can be divided into internal and external messaging. The method chosen should be tailored to each audience and should educate the audience on the organization's mission, strategies, programs, and activities. To do this, it is important to identify the audience and message to be communicated and develop the marketing tools to deliver the message. Whether the communication is designed for recruitment, requests for proposals (RFPs), or informing or educating the internal audience, there are a few fundamental guidelines to follow: know your audience, ensure all communication has consistent themes, verify the accuracy of any data and explain any inconsistencies, and understand why you need this message conveyed.

Know Your Audience

An understanding of the targeted reader or participant is vital, and an intrinsic part of this understanding is appreciating the motive for consuming the material. Is the material geared toward students? Is it focused on one particular aspect of recruiting, for example, a scholarship? Are you targeting a particular demographic (women, LGBT, etc.)? Is the marketing tool in response to a client or potential client request? How do you think the information will be used? Is this for internal eyes only? What are your internal marketing needs? Is there a need to educate the company or firm about the diversity efforts? Are you documenting activities? Are you encouraging people to participate? What would motivate the internal audience to read the material? Why?

Ensure All Communications Have Consistent Themes

Regardless of the audience, all marketing materials must have the same fundamental message regarding the organization's diversity efforts. The mission statement, philosophy, and principles must be communicated in ways that reinforce the organization's diversity commitment and premise. The reason for investing in diversity efforts is the same whether the audience is internal or external. There are always options to expand upon aspects of the theme that are tailored to a particular audience, but when reviewed collectively, all communications and marketing tools must convey the same fundamental message.

Verify the Accuracy of the Data

Marketing materials will often rely on data that is important or well-known to the particular audience. For example, marketing to law students must be done with the knowledge that law students rely on National Association for Law Placement (NALP) data, which is based on head count. NALP categorizes data by particular demographics for each law firm office; for example, they do not report or track equity partner status, as opposed to Vault, which does track and report equity partner status. When communicating demographic information on the organization's U.S. offices, for example, and not just the main office of the firm, be sure to use data that will not confuse your reader or appear to be inaccurate. Also, if your materials convey equity status numbers, be careful that the numbers you report in your materials are easy to explain if the numbers appear to be inconsistent. Sometimes, equity status is based on full time equivalent (FTE), not head count, and therefore there may appear to be a discrepancy. Data may also change after the date it is reported. When marketing to clients, if relevant, be sure to acknowledge and reconcile the issue of different databases (FTE versus head count) and reporting dates.

Determine Why You Are Communicating

What is the point of the communication? Who is your audience, and why are you developing a marketing tool for them? Is it information that you must provide continuously at events? Is your goal to educate your audience with a one-page informational sheet? Are you seeking to persuade your audience that you have a good diversity program? Are you trying to promote a specific segment of your organization? Are you trying to encourage the audience to do something specific, such as apply for a scholarship, attend an event, learn more from a website, or become educated or persuaded? Are you establishing that you are an attractive employer?

Once the fundamental essence and audience has been determined, an important consideration is whether this is an internal or an external communication. Internal communications are intended for internal audiences only. External communications are designed with an understanding that unfamiliar audiences will be receiving the information and internal protocols may be required before publishing the communication.

Internal Communications

There will be a need to provide general communications to internal audiences only. Internal communications can contain more informal information that does not require explanation, such as internal acronyms or shared information. An example is acronym for a leadership group, such as ExComm for executive committee or SDC for strategic diversity committee, or a reference to the managing partner by name, but not by title. Examples of internal communications are affinity group newsletters for their group and members of the firm, an annual diversity report, monthly internal communications, updates, welcome messages, reports on progress or activities such as retreats, and reports.

External Communications

External communications will be forever in the public domain. Always check to determine if there are firm or company protocols prior to publishing information outside the organization. External communications provide basic information that you want to share with the external world to accomplish a specific purpose. Examples of external communications are one-page information sheets, annual reviews, language and information for RFPs, and specific marketing materials.

As you develop your communications tools, keep in mind your ultimate goal. Ask whether the communication is designed to inform, educate, promote, persuade, or some combination thereof. While there is a fine line between informing and educating, there are distinctions, as well as important differences between promoting and persuading. It is crucial to appreciate that diversity initiatives and programs are often asked to do all of these things in many aspects of the programming and communications.

Five Important Points Regarding Communication of the Diversity Initiative

1. *Inform*: This is the most basic reason to communicate the philosophy, mission, and function of the organization's diversity initiative. It communicates what you do, how you do it, and who does what and when. An example of this kind of communication is the language in a welcome kit that provides information on the diversity programs and allows new employees to opt into affinity groups. Other examples are language that describes the diversity program in RFPs or proposals or information posted on the front diversity page of the organization's website.
2. *Educate*: This takes information to the next level. Beyond the what, who, and when (including why diversity is important and

what it means), educational materials provide the answers to what the diversity program is doing that is important, why it is important, and how it matters. This type of communication can also provide fundamental diversity education, such as information on subject matters that are relevant. Examples of this kind of communication are affinity group newsletters; one-page recruitment materials, including those that target specific demographics such as women, lawyers of color, or LGBT attorneys; annual publications that provide a review of programs and activities; and secondary pages on the website that give more detail on the diversity programs.

3. *Promote*: These materials are designed to get the reader to act. They can advertise an event or program. Such materials serve as marketing tools to provide information as a foundation for an understanding of the event or activity that is being promoted. Invitations to an affinity group event or to promote the women's retreat are examples of this type of communication. Marketing materials designed for particular affinity groups, such as a brochure marketing to African American attorneys for the National Bar Association's Commercial Law Conference, can also fall in this category.
4. *Persuade*: This type of communication combines all of the above to inform, educate, promote, and ultimately convince the reader. These materials are used mostly in award applications as well as proposals to the firm or company management. Examples include language used for awards, such as the NAFE Best Firms for Women Survey, MCCA's Employers of Choice, Yale Top Ten Firms for Women, the 40 Under 40 awards, the National Organization for Women, local bar associations, ABA awards, and others.
5. *Communicate*: There are many different formats and styles that can be used to communicate an organization's diversity and inclusion message, but simple and short is always prudent. However, there are times when more is better because of the depth and breadth of the communications tool.

Forms of Effective Communication for Your Diversity Message

- One-page sheets on
  - The diversity program, which can be used in recruitment and general information dissemination
  - Affinity groups, either individually or collectively, which can be used at affinity bar association conferences that target these particular groups, i.e., women, LGBT, etc.
- Annual review: Similar to the annual reports published by corporations, this is a review of the annual goals, activities, programs and state of affairs. It is usually several pages long.
- Periodic newsletters that target a specific group, like an affinity group. This is designed to provide updates and information, sometimes with a spotlight on a member and short blurbs about activities.
- An internal annual report that captures and quantifies the business, programs, and activities of the organization's diversity and inclusion efforts. This kind of tool is in a chronicling format, rather than a narrative description. It should contain reports, budget, activities, publications, ads, and any other materials that record efforts, results, and other activities for the year.
- Template language for marketing materials such as RFPs, pitch materials, etc.
- Materials used for orientation, associate conferences, and attorney retreats.

For ease of access and in an effort to advance internal green/environmental initiatives, all materials should reside virtually on the internal intranet or the external website, where appropriate, including periodic newsletters, the annual report, and marketing language. Of course, all communications should be housed virtually and made available internally or externally, whichever is appropriate.

Some materials need to be in hard copy for the particular dissemination required. If you are attending conferences and the organization has a booth or table, it is always good to have materials available. This allows your message to be received if the table is too crowded or unattended at that moment. Also, hard copies of certain materials, such as the annual review or recruiting brochure, should be made available as table magazines in the organization's reception area.

Working with Your Marketing Department

Including your marketing professionals in your diversity communications strategy is a necessary and important consideration. First, the responsibility for ensuring your firm's diversity goals and messages are an integral aspect of all communications should be a shared responsibility with the marketing and diversity teams. Working in partnership with your marketing professionals can advance your organization's diversity goals in several ways; for example, the marketing department can be extremely instrumental in identifying opportunities in local and national media. Utilizing relationships to collaborate and advance the practice expertise and accomplishment of diverse attorneys, partners in particular, is one way that the marketing department can contribute to advancing media goals. There are many ways to work with the marketing department and it is critical to work together to determine how your organization's marketing professionals can best contribute to the organization's diversity goals.

See Chapter 6 on Inside the Organization for additional discussion on working with the marketing department.

What You Should Know

- You should always find a way to communicate your mission, message, and methods. It should always be accessible and easy to find.
- Always choose content over style, substance over form if you have to choose. In other words, if your budget for communications is small, invest in telling your story as opposed to presenting a pretty picture. A simple one-page informational sheet is better than a glossy picture-laden book that does not show substance.
- Know your message. Decide what you want your audience to know. Then tell them. Our diversity and efforts are moving along. . . . We need your support. . . . Recruiting is successful because of your efforts . . . Our attorney are super stars . . . Know your story, why you want to tell it, and then make it clear.

CHAPTER 6

INSIDE THE ORGANIZATION: BEWARE OF THE SILOS

Or you cannot do it alone

Overview

The goals of the organization's diversity and inclusion efforts are interwoven in almost every aspect of the organization. The diversity professional must interact with many departments, committees, and teams on a regular basis. It is crucial to appreciate the intersection of these areas with the organization's diversity and inclusion goals. In all situations, there can be value added from an interdepartmental team approach.

It is important is to first identify the areas and departments, their intersection, and the value added through a strategic relationship. Some of the obvious strategic relationships include recruitment, professional development, associate evaluations, compensation, marketing and communications, information technology, and human resources and finance. Following are suggested strategies for the development and maintenance of these relationships with key departments.

Information Technology

The diversity professional should communicate and interact regularly with the information technology team, including developing an appreciation and understanding of the institution's software functions and limitations and how they can best serve the needs of the diversity professional. This may include intranet development and use, listservs, data management, mailboxes, reporting programs, and others. This area can be especially helpful in the development and implementation of new, creative, and innovative products and initiatives to advance the organization's diversity and inclusion efforts.

Human Resources and Finance

Interaction with the human resources and finance departments often centers on data collection, but these departments also have other resources and functions. Typically, these departments collect and store data in department-specific software that is needed for surveys and other internal and external requests. Efficient communication with these departments can facilitate open discussions and a clear understanding of the available resources that may be helpful to advance diversity and inclusion goals. Also, the recruiting function may be housed in human resources, and budgeting usually resides in finance. The presence of these critical diversity functions creates a need for a strong and strategic relationship with these departments.

Compensation Committee

If the diversity professional serves at a senior level, he or she may be involved in compensation communications and decisions at the associate and partner levels. Because the compensation process varies in each organization, and is often of a sensitive nature, the diversity professional's role will vary. The organization should review policies, practices, and strategies to ensure that diverse perspectives and views are incorporated in the evaluation and compensation process. Diversity awareness education and training for the compensation committee members should also be developed and implemented. For further discussion, please see Chapter 2 on accountability.

Marketing and Communications

This is a relationship where each department is a client for the other at times. The diversity professional is an internal client of the marketing department when he or she needs materials, such as ads, literature, signs, promotional materials, and so on. The marketing department is an internal client of the diversity professional or team when it needs information for RFPs, client pitches, and organizational marketing materials, including advice and counsel on target market publications. An effective working relationship can result in creative branding for the organization's diversity efforts, effective marketing materials, and strategic use of diversity in firm efforts as well as marketing the organization's strategic diversity efforts. For further discussion, please see Chapter 5 on communications.

Recruitment

Diversity and inclusion goals and recruitment goals intersect on many levels. From on-campus student recruitment to lateral attorney hiring, there must be strong communications and programmatic interaction. Such interactions may include attending on-campus events, providing input on student organizations and involvement, participating in interviews and hiring committee meetings and decisions, programmatic development for effective recruitment practices, strategizing on job fairs and executive recruiters, active involvement in strategy sessions on diversity hiring, and participation in preparing and reviewing recruiting materials. Interactions may also include shared department meetings, training (such as diversity or interviewing techniques training), joint attendance at recruiting and diversity conferences or seminars, and working with internal affinity groups to assist and participate in recruiting efforts. Please see Chapter 7 for further discussion on recruiting.

Professional Development

This is an important relationship that intersects with the organization's diversity goals; it is a key department for addressing retention issues. An open and strong relationship with this department is critical in order to determine how the organization's professional development strategy will support attorneys with diverse backgrounds individually, collectively, and within the overall larger group. The diversity professional should work closely with professional development to raise issues such as diversity goals being an essential consideration of how the department provides resources, education, and support, or specific programming for the professional development of attorneys with diverse backgrounds, and provide input, education, data, recommendations, and ideas. Advancing diversity goals can be the catalyst for the identification of challenges, opportunities, and solutions in some of the organization's systems. This will ultimately be to the benefit of all. Diversity and inclusion efforts can be the model for pilot programs that may subsequently be implemented for the larger community. Please see Chapter 9 for further discussion on professional development and retention.

EVALUATION, DEVELOPMENT, AND TALENT MANAGEMENT

The diversity professional should always be involved with and aware of the associate development process, including formal and informal evaluations for attorneys from diverse backgrounds. If the position is at a senior level, the diversity professional should have access to all information before and throughout the evaluation process. The diversity team should work together with the talent management or associate development teams to be proactive in anticipating any interventions, whether positive or negative. Each department should be aware if there are issues with performance, hours, ethics, and protocols. Regular communications throughout the year on these and other matters will encourage and permit proactive intervention and avoid the need for the diversity professional to intervene in a crisis management situation. For further discussion, please see Chapter 9 on professional development and retention.

An important aspect of developing strategic relationships is to share and candidly discuss the needs of the diversity team and efforts and how a particular department or team can contribute to the advancement of the organization's diversity and inclusion goals. Internal resources may be limited; thus, developing open avenues for communication and the exchange of ideas is valuable and will facilitate support and collaboration.

What You Should Know

Remember, diversity is everyone's business, and it is in everyone's business.

- You cannot do it alone. You must have allies—not friends, not diversity zealots—allies. You need them.
- Know and understand your stakeholders. Know who they are and what is important to them. Find ways to connect with them that increases your awareness of their roles and responsibilities as well as their awareness of your role and responsibilities. Invite them to your conferences and seek to attend some of theirs.
- Volunteer to work on some of their projects.
- Share some of your internal best practices or short cuts you have learned to be more efficient.
- Share your staff for events.
- Act like a partner. Invite them to become a partner.

CHAPTER 7

COMPREHENSIVE RECRUITMENT

Or from strategic to grass roots: an approach to find and hire

Overview

Diversity recruiting initiatives are often the hallmark of a diversity program. For the diversity professional, it can be the panacea for achieving short- and long-term diversity and inclusion goals. There are three critical elements the diversity professional should consider when developing a diversity recruiting initiative: strategy, strategy, and strategy. Every aspect of diversity recruiting should be strategic. The diversity professional must work hand-in-hand with the recruiting professionals and hiring committee to develop and implement the strategic plan. He or she must remain vigilant in advancing the business case for implementing a diversity recruiting strategy and linking it with the organization's overall business objectives and goals. A few questions to consider include:

- What are your short- and long-term diversity recruiting goals?
- What are your priorities?
- What are your parameters? Are all positions included in the diversity efforts?
- How can you utilize current recruiting practices to implement your diversity recruiting initiatives?
- How will you measure success? Keep in mind that it is not enough to just look at the numbers.

- What are your resources (budget, human capital)?
- Who are your champions?
- What are your external goals?

To get started:

- Perform an assessment of past hiring practices: determine what has been successful and, equally important, unsuccessful.
- Review hiring policies and procedures. Are they clearly stated? Objective? Transparent?
- Track the diversity of candidates you are seeing: on-campus recruitment, call-back interviews, offers, acceptances. Oftentimes this data is estimated and may be based on visual and resume data and not on self-identification information. It is recommended that the data be compiled in the aggregate, rather than individually.
- Establish a recruiting plan: entry level, lateral, outreach. An important aspect of developing strategic relationships is to share and candidly discuss the needs of the diversity team and efforts and how such department or team can contribute to the advancement of the organization's diversity and inclusion goals. As internal resources may be limited, developing open avenues for communication and the exchange of ideas is valuable and will facilitate support and collaboration.
- Develop and implement unconscious bias training or programming for members of the recruiting and hiring teams.

Building a critical mass of diverse attorneys is essential to achieving the diversity and inclusion goals of an organization. This chapter will discuss diversity recruiting strategies, including on-campus and lateral recruiting practices, scholarship and intern programs, and diversity pipeline efforts.

Recruiting Strategy

Currently, most law firms hire directly from law schools and receive the single largest influx of new lawyers through their summer associate recruiting process. Implementing a diversity recruiting strategy should be a continuing effort that does not start and end with the fall on-campus recruiting season. Recruitment is a broad and ongoing process that requires consistency. It is important to start by examining and utilizing your existing recruiting program. Ask how diversity and inclusion recruiting goals can be weaved into what the organization is already doing. This is an effective and efficient way to build and expand the organization's diversity recruiting initiative so that it is in line with its culture. Drastic changes in hiring policies may not be well-received and may be rejected in organizations that have relied on a "time-honored" system and practice for many years (which has been largely perceived as being rooted in a meritocracy). Working closely with members of the recruiting and hiring committee or team as part of the process is essential when revising diversity recruiting practices.

A few words about recruiting goals: An important goal of a diversity recruiting initiative specifically at law firms is to have a diverse summer associate class—in the broadest sense, leading to a diverse first-year associate class. Diversity in terms of law schools represented, backgrounds, areas of interest, and cultural experiences, as well as diverse racial and ethnic representation, members of the LGBT community, persons with disabilities, and gender and gender identity all represent important aspects of diversity. Remember the veterans as well.

A common criticism regarding diversity recruiting is that it will somehow lead to a lessening of the organization's hiring standards or candidate qualifications. This is certainly not the goal or the desired result. Diversity recruiting initiatives should include goals, set timetables, and metrics to evaluate progress. Law firms and legal departments should review overall hiring policies and procedures to make sure current practices are consistent with the diversity strategy of the entire organization, and encourage and support diversity in the hiring process. Consider revising polices when working with recruiters to require a diverse slate of candidates when interviewing and hiring for all positions within the organization.

A similar practice was successfully implemented by the National Football League (NFL) in 2003 as part of a diversity initiative to increase the number of ethnic minority NFL coaches. Referred to as the "Rooney Rule," this practice was conceived by Dan Rooney, owner of the Pittsburgh

Steelers and then chair of the NFL Diversity Committee. The rule requires that at least one ethnic minority candidate be included among the slate of candidates being interviewed for all new senior and coaching positions. In general, the initiative has been viewed as a success. Between 2003 and the celebration of its ten-year anniversary in 2013, 17 teams have named either an ethnic minority head coach or general manager, according to the Bleacher Report. (Bleacherreport.com, Mike Freeman, October 24, 2013, "The Rooney Rule 10 Years Later") Although there has been controversy surrounding rule implementation, the Rooney Rule is a clear statement of the commitment by the NFL to expand and advance diversity within the coaching ranks.

Be clear and transparent about the organization's qualifications for all candidates. Raising awareness regarding the use of clearly articulated, objective hiring qualifications requires a review and interpretation of the standards for all candidates, not just the "diverse" candidates. Reviewing hiring policies with an eye towards furthering the organization's goals is helpful to identify and unlock vague language. For example, terms such as "dynamic," "talented," "well-credentialed," "good fit," and "having the qualities necessary to succeed" can, and often do, lend themselves to subjective interpretation by the interviewer and fail to state clear examples of whether a candidate is or is not qualified for the position.

To get started, first take a look at your historical hiring practices and results. It is helpful to perform an audit of past hires to identify the level of diversity in past hiring decisions and the criteria used in making such decisions. It is important to note the schools where you have had a successful diversity recruiting experience. Often it is found that modifications of and exceptions to the written hiring standards have been applied in cases of "nondiverse" candidates. Ask questions: Did he or she meet our grade point average requirement? Was there something else about his or her experience or skills that impacted the hiring decision? As noted in Chapter 14 on data collection, collecting data is critical to developing and implementing solutions.

Clearly, no one single criterion can predict the success a law student will have at a law firm or other organization. We often think we are relying on our professional experience and other seemingly objective factors to guide us, but science has told us that such past experiences are not necessarily reliable. Hiring committees and recruiters should participate in diversity education awareness programs that focus on the recognition and elimination of implicit bias. This topic is expansive and it is important to include this aspect of education in one's recruiting strategy. Diversity awareness programs and training are discussed further in Chapter 11.

Several studies and authorities, including the recent book by Howard Ross, *Everyday Bias: Identifying and Navigating Unconscious Judgements in Our Daily Lives*, give an excellent overview of the neuroscience, stating that we cannot rely on just good intentions. Unintentional bias plays a significant part in how we make decisions. Candid and open discussions with experts in this area are extremely helpful in the raising awareness of the individuals who are charged with making the hiring decisions and members of the recruiting department, as well as the policies and practices used.

Diversity recruiting goals can be achieved through many initiatives, including:

- On-campus summer associate recruiting
- Diversity job fairs
- School considerations
- Scholarship programs
- Law student summer intern programs
- Lateral recruiting
- Diversity pipeline initiatives
- Bar association and nonprofit organization sponsored internship programs

On-Campus Recruiting: A Grassroots Approach

On-campus summer associate recruiting is still the traditional method of recruiting new lawyers to law firms through the law school on-campus interviewing process and is typically led by the organization's recruiting department. Attempting to increase the diversity of the summer associate class through the on-campus system is essential, but without a thoughtful strategy, it can be arbitrary and may not be beneficial in terms of advancing your diversity recruiting goals.

One of the most effective methods of on-campus recruiting is to develop a grassroots initiative directly with the school, career services and admissions offices, student organizations, and students. Be present and be frequent, with early and frequent contact. It is not enough to just show up for the fall recruiting season, which now starts in August at many law schools. It is critical to have a presence throughout the year and to get to know the students, including the leaders and members of the law school affinity groups, such as the African American law student groups, Latino law student groups, Asian law student groups, women's groups, LGBT groups, and others. Getting to know the leaders and members of the student groups is essential to developing a relationship with the students the organization is seeking to recruit. In addition to adding sincerity and greater legitimacy to the diversity recruiting efforts from the school and student perspective, it will bring one in touch with the individual students, helping to preidentify those who are interested in working in the areas of law that your organization practices and living in the geographic regions where the organization's offices are located. All are important aspects of the process.

Hosting programs to showcase the organization and sponsoring informal receptions on campus or nearby at a local restaurant for first- and second-year law students to discuss practical topics, such as resume writing, how to be a good summer associate, the dos and don'ts of social media, or advice on getting an A in law school, are important ways of reaching students directly and assisting them in being successful in school and ultimately at your organization. The cost and time are minimal, but the return on the investment can be expansive. *It is important, however, to be aware of the National Association for Law Placement (NALP) recruiting rules and guidelines regarding the timing of certain outreach.* Although the diversity professional or team must have input and participate in developing the organization's diversity recruiting strategy, on-campus recruiting efforts should be led by the organization's recruiting team, because diversity recruitment efforts should not differ from the organization's overall recruiting policies and practices.

Often members of the diversity and inclusion and recruiting teams can assist in leading on-campus discussions and cultivating relationships with the students. Clearly, there will be certain discussions for which you will need to have the presence and participation of a hiring partner or other senior person at the organization; however, that will not be the case for all meetings. For example, a topic such as "how to develop an effective study guide" may be best discussed by a junior lawyer of the firm. Participation should take place at all levels of the firm. Including the assistance of your prior 2L summer associates to participate in 1L recruiting at their schools can be very successful, because they are the perfect ambassadors for your organization if their experience has been positive. A student's personal experience cannot be duplicated by associates and partners and is always of interest to the other students—they like and trust hearing from other students similarly situated. For example, women, attorneys of color, and openly LGBT attorneys should discuss with ease and candor their insights and perspectives regarding their respective experiences at the organization, as it is helpful to demystify and clarify experiences.

A grassroots strategy is time-intensive and may not be possible, at least initially, at every school where you are recruiting. In partnership with the recruiting team, the diversity professional or team should identify a limited number of schools to focus on when implementing this type of in-depth initiative. These schools should have been identified as important by recruitment. This strategy can take several seasons to build and nurture and should not been seen as an instant fix.

After the candidates to be interviewed have been identified, the on-campus interviews completed, and the call-back process and extension of offers is complete, it is critical to have a plan for a comprehensive follow-up. Did the students have the opportunity to meet a diverse group of attorneys at the firm? Were the students included in any events hosted by the firm or sponsored by any expressed affinity group interests? Was there outreach by the hiring committee? Have lawyers from the interested practice areas expressed by the students reached out to the candidates? Such efforts will demonstrate the importance you place on bringing the students to the firm and your belief in their success. Although dinners and parties are nice, one-on-one discussions with practicing attorneys at the firm are key to the success of your diversity recruiting efforts.

DIVERSITY JOB FAIRS

In addition to on-campus recruiting, many organizations host or sponsor diversity job and career fairs in which law firms and many other legal organizations participate. The events may be organized to attract both law students and experienced attorneys. An important benefit of job fairs is the diversity of interests, backgrounds, and skills among the attendees. Often law firms or legal departments may meet candidates from schools or regions where they do not, or due to restricted budgets cannot, recruit. Through job fairs they will have the opportunity to meet interested candidates whom they otherwise may not have met. The candidates' skill levels and qualifications will vary greatly at a job fair, and therefore make it more challenging to identify candidates for positions at your organization; it is an excellent opportunity for you to share and expand your organization's diversity brand. Further, it is an opportunity to network, identify interested candidates, and supplement your recruiting efforts.

DIVERSITY SCHOLARSHIPS

Diversity scholarship programs can be an excellent recruiting tool and an important pipeline resource. Scholarship programs vary widely, but all require meticulous planning and execution. Thoughts to consider when developing a scholarship program include:

- What are your program goals?
- Will the focus include long-term diversity pipeline goals?
- Will there be a time limit on the program?
- How will the program be funded?
- Who will be included on the scholarship selection committee?
- What will the scholarship amount be?

- How will the scholarship amount be distributed?
- Will other organizations participate or partner in the scholarship program?
- Who will be eligible to apply for the scholarship?
- Will there be criteria for participation (such as a requirement to participate in the sponsor's summer intern program)?
- Will the scholarship program provide other benefits (such as internship opportunities)?
- What will the process for reviewing and selecting scholarship recipients be?
- What internal and external resources will be needed to support the program?

Once the program structure has been determined and put in place, careful consideration and planning are needed in the development of the roll-out plan. The diversity professional should work with members of the marketing team to develop the roll-out plan, including creation of a scholarship page on the organization's website, use of social media, outreach to organizations, such as bar associations and schools, and the preparation of materials describing the program. Consideration also should be given to scholarship recipient follow-up, such as an alumni program to promote ongoing relationships and to keep the scholars in touch with the organization. Scholarship programs can be labor intensive and will require meticulous and in-depth pre-planning and implementation.

School Considerations

Selecting the law schools where you will recruit on-campus is an important consideration and should be determined by members of the hiring committee and recruiting department and include input from the diversity professional or team. Many of the top 20 law schools have a broad range of ethnic, racial, gender, and LGBT diversity among the student population, as well as culture, language capabilities, and other areas of diversity. Regional schools that could serve as geographic feeder schools to a particular office in your organization are an important consideration. Consider the need to cast a wider net if the student body is not particularly diverse or you have not had successful diversity recruiting experiences at such schools. Further, there is a great deal of competition at all law schools, in particular the top-rated schools, for students in the top 10 to 15 percent of the class, and even more so for the diverse candidates. This is another reason to cast a wider net when identifying the schools that will have a priority focus in your diversity recruiting initiative.

Recruiting professionals are excellent resources and the diversity professional must utilize their expertise when developing the diversity recruiting strategy and implementing initiatives and programs. The diversity professional or team should not function in a recruiting silo. Members of the diversity team should participate and play an active role in the recruiting process, including attending dinners and receptions for all candidates, not just for the diverse candidates. It is important for your organization that the students see and recognize your diversity efforts and brand as an important business initiative that benefits the entire organization.

Student affinity groups will often seek out law firm, law department, or other organizational participation, particularly in terms of program events and sponsorship opportunities. Often the requests will be plentiful and can challenge organizational resources, both in terms of lawyer participation and budget. Evaluate each sponsorship request to determine if it furthers your recruiting goals and is beneficial to the students, as well as your organization. Questions to ask of the student organizers include: How many students do they anticipate will participate in the event? How many attended last year's event? Do they expect the students to be 2Ls or 3Ls? How many other sponsors will be there? How many attorneys and firm representatives can you send to participate? Will there be a formal program, and if so, can members of your organization participate as presenters? Answers to these questions can help you balance the benefits of the investment opportunity and the resources needed to respond.

Participating in student affinity group events prior to the date of the on-campus interviews will give you an added opportunity to become reacquainted with students met during the prior recruiting season (and who are now 2Ls) and the opportunity to preidentify any student you would like to interview who may not be on your schedule. Of course, it is always helpful to one's recruiting efforts to have close and frequent student contact during the school year, not just during on-campus recruiting time. Programming that showcases the organization and furthers its brand is important, as this can assist in distinguishing the organization from others at a time when students are likely overwhelmed with information.

If there are students who worked with one's organization during their 1L or 2L summer and have accepted or are considering an offer to return to the organization, there should be outreach to include and utilize them during fall recruiting efforts at their school. They should be invited to attend the organization's on-campus receptions, as well as speak with other students regarding their experiences at the organization. This may sound extremely fundamental; however, if the recruiting department and diversity team are not working well together, this is something that can easily be missed. Gaining multiple benefits from a single source is crucial. Attending a student affinity group event hosted by several school affinity groups can give you access to a larger group of students, rather than one group, which will have a smaller number of student participants.

Spring Recruitment

At the end of the fall recruiting season, the organization should be ready to implement its spring diversity recruitment strategy. Outreach to 1L student affinity groups, including program participation, is critical. This is the time to get to know the students who will be actively recruited in the fall. It is the time to develop relationships, and learn more about what the students are looking for and, to a certain extent, how to assist. Further, it is a good time to get feedback on what programs and initiatives are helpful and what may need additional thought and work. Although the fervor of fall recruitment need not move over into the spring, considerable time and resources should be given to developing your diversity pipeline for the following recruiting season. Keeping the students close by staying in touch during the spring and summer will help you to broaden and direct your diversity recruiting outreach in the fall.

Insight from an Industry Expert

Some Tips from a Recruitment Specialist, NALP Executive Director James Leipold

With respect to recruiting law students, James Leipold states that it is important to build relationships with schools over time so that the law firm has an identity, presence, and reputation on campus. Students actually learn the most about potential employers from each other and from students who are returning from summer work experiences. A firm must always look locally, at the law schools around it.

Leipold emphasizes: Figure out all the ways you can build relationships by providing attorneys to speak on campus and reaching out to minority student organizations like the Black American Law Students Association (BALSA). Determine how the law firm can be of service or work collaboratively with the student organizations, whether it's through funding or providing speakers. On the topic of 1L summer associate programs, Leipold suggested that it makes a lot of sense to think about having a 1L diversity summer program, because it introduces the students early on to your firm. "I've seen 1L programs be very effective and they can be done collaboratively with a client and include joint programming," states Leipold.

For those with 1L summer hiring, you can begin reaching out to students after Dec. 1st.

Although legal departments often do not hire directly out of law school, the implementation of a summer legal intern program is helpful in introducing students to the in-house corporate perspective and establishing early relationships. Insight from an interview with Nate Saint-Victor, Executive Director at Morgan Stanley, describes its innovative ten-week 1L summer intern diversity program, including an Alumni Connect program, mentoring efforts, CLE programming, and creative partnerships. The full interview can be read at the end of this chapter.

Lateral Recruiting

Lateral recruiting can be cyclical and often focuses on specific areas of practice; however, like the Rooney Rule, the diversity professional should work with the recruiting department or outside recruiter to implement organizational policies that encourage obtaining a diverse slate of candidates for all positions the organization is seeking to fill. The lateral recruiting market is an excellent way to supplement the organization's diversity recruiting objectives.

Firms often use professional recruiters to assist in identifying and locating attorneys to fill the specific needs of practice areas or departments. In every case, it should be clear to the recruiter that he or she must present a diverse slate of candidates for the position, with a focus on groups that are underrepresented in the organization. Online recruiting utilizing Internet employment sites can be helpful, but may yield a very large number of interested resumes. It is important when reviewing the resumes and narrowing the candidate list to be diligent in making sure they are being reviewed with an objective eye. As noted above, unintentional bias can have a significant impact on how one makes decisions. Incorporating lateral recruiting efforts as part of the overall diversity strategy can assist in furthering diversity goals, in particular when examining data within the organization that raises concerns with respect to underrepresented groups.

Lateral recruiting opportunities can be linked with bar association programs, diversity conferences, CLE programs, and by recommendations based on past working relationships. Proactive lateral recruiting will help make sure the needs of your organization, practice, office and diversity goals are being met. Every lawyer you meet is a potential lateral hire.

Insight from an Industry Expert

Merle Vaughn, Managing Director, Major, Lindsey & Africa

With Respect to Recruiting Laterals: The Mechanics of a Targeted Diversity Search

A *targeted search* is one in which the recruiter works with the law firm or law department to determine a specific area in which they'd like to add lawyers. "We create a list of lawyers who meet the criteria either from our database or from other resources. The law firm will take the list, vet it internally and then let us know who they want us to contact," states Merle Vaughn.

A *retained search* is a search in which the law firms pays the recruiter in advance to initiate the search; regardless of whether or not the person is placed, the recruiter is entitled to keep the fee for the services rendered, at least for running the search. Retained searches are always exclusive. Vaughn emphasizes that a *nonretained exclusive search* means that the recruiter is not being compensated up front, but the firm agrees not to conduct an independent search or work with another recruiter.

Vaughn describes how you cull the list for lawyers with whom the firm may have already been in discussions. "That would be called a carve-out list. The firm would give us a list of people with whom they've already spoken and it's possible to carve those people out."

Remember James Leipold's Advice for Recruiting Law Students

- Relationships with law schools help to establish a brand and reputation.
- Students get their primary information from each other.
- Adding value to student organizations helps build a brand-hosting interviewing sessions, reviewing resumes, sponsoring events, etc.
- 1L programs can help early identification of candidates and help build your brand earlier with students.

Remember Merle Vaughn's Advice for Recruiting Laterals

Consider a targeted search, whether exclusive or not. Before you do so, create a list of lawyers you have already contacted and discuss that list with the recruiter to identify the criteria for the candidates.

Insight: Diversity and Inclusion Are Business Imperatives

Interview with Nate Saint-Victor, Executive Director, Morgan Stanley

Following is a Q&A with Nate Saint-Victor, Executive Director at Morgan Stanley and Chair of the Diversity and Inclusion Committee within the Morgan Stanley Legal and Compliance Division. Saint-Victor discusses the Morgan Stanley diversity and inclusion summer intern program, the new Alumni Connect program, the 14 subcommittees and 170 members of the diversity and inclusion committee, pipeline efforts, advice for diversity professionals, and more.

Q: What are the missions and objectives of the Morgan Stanley Legal and Compliance Diversity and Inclusion Committee?

A: Our firm has a strong belief that our culture is our most important tool and that in order for us to be successful as a business enterprise we have to have diverse teams, and we have to demonstrate inclusive behaviors that align with our firm's core values, which are (1) putting clients first, (2) leading with exceptional ideas, (3) doing the right thing, and (4) giving back. We believe that a diverse, inclusive workforce is an opportunity for our clients, our shareholders, as well as our employees. The Morgan Stanley Legal and Compliance Division's Diversity and Inclusion Committee (LCDDIC) seeks to fulfill the firm's mission by: maintaining an environment where diversity is respected and encouraged; leveraging our differences—which include the full range of social and cultural identities, organizational roles, and perspectives—to enhance our effectiveness; and

Continued

Insight: Diversity and Inclusion Are Business Imperatives *Continued*

increasing diversity and inclusion at every level of our Division and more broadly within the legal and compliance profession.

Q: How do these objectives align with your recruiting efforts?

A: Quite frankly, as a global franchise, our leadership will rest on the talent of our people and their ability to advise and serve our clients in a first-class way. We know the diversity of our people is one of our greatest strengths, as we must have the broadest possible knowledge of the global markets in which we operate.

One of our recruiting practices within the Legal and Compliance Division is to publish opportunities with a variety of different affinity groups and organizations that can share jobs with diverse talent. To name a few, Corporate Counsel Women of Color, the Minority Corporate Counsel Association, and the New York City Bar Association, which has a strong diversity and inclusion office. We also look at organizations like the Council of Urban Professionals, which also has access to a large group of talented individuals.

Something else we've done in the past and we look to do from time to time is to use recruiters focused on identifying a diverse group of applicants.

We also conduct exploratory interviews when we identify top diverse talent. Once identified, we'll bring them in for conversations so that we're getting to know them even if there's not a specific opportunity that is currently available. We know that by developing relationships with such talent we're in a better place to be ready to approach them once an opportunity arises.

Lastly, our recruiting strategies occasionally tie into some of the programming that we do as well. For example, we partnered with the New York chapter of the Association of Corporate Counsel (ACC Greater New York), as well as the Metropolitan Black Bar Association (MBBA) to host a successful career and compliance forum for diverse professionals that were interested in learning about compliance opportunities within financial services. As a result, we were able to identify talented professionals for several roles within our Division.

Q: Can you describe your summer legal intern program?

A: Since 2003, the Legal and Compliance Division at Morgan Stanley has offered a competitive ten-week paid internship to diverse first-year law stu- dents which has now expanded to include college students. Each year, we interview candidates from New York area law schools and several other select northeastern law schools. Candidates can submit their resumes directly through our website. It's a rigorous selection process. We receive several hundred applications, but it's a small program of about 10-12 interns. The program gives interns the opportunity to learn about being a legal or compliance professional within the financial services industry through substantive work from various practice areas within the Legal and Compliance Division, and also by meeting with business people during branch office visits and trading-floor tours.

As part of the robust program, we partner on programming with outside counsel giving interns the opportunity to interact with attorneys and summer associates at law firms during planned activities and training sessions. They also meet with senior attorneys and compliance professionals within Legal and Compliance through weekly "Lunch and Learn" sessions.

Each intern is assigned to a senior lawyer or compliance professional who serves as his or her mentor throughout the summer. This helps ensure a complete transition and that they're really maximizing the ten-week internship that they have with us.

In 2013, we launched our AlumniConnect program, through which we've established a database and opportunities to communicate with alumni of our summer intern program over the past 11 years. Through this program, we invite former summer interns to come back to Morgan Stanley for an annual summer reception and other substantive or networking events so they stay familiar with the Firm. We also invite them back for continuing legal education (CLE) sessions so that they can get some of their legal education training at work with Morgan Stanley Legal and Compliance professionals. By nurturing relationships with these alumni and helping to enrich their development as professionals, Morgan Stanley

Continued

Insight: Diversity and Inclusion Are Business Imperatives *Continued*

will stay top of mind as opportunities may arise as they develop their experience in financial services.

Q: What has the feedback been regarding your initiatives?

A: We're very proud of our initiatives and feel strongly that we've committed talent, intellectual capital, and resources to develop a culture that embraces diversity and inclusion. We know that there remains much work to be done and, in an effort to be vanguards and remain cutting-edge, we continue to reinvent ourselves, regularly re-evaluating each of our efforts and drawing from industry research and analysis. We challenge ourselves every day so that we can try to get smarter and better every year.

In terms of feedback, we get a lot through the way the Legal and Compliance Division Diversity and Inclusion Committee is structured. I chair the Committee and report directly to our Chief Operations Officer and the Chief Legal Officer oversees all activities. The committee has 170 members, including 12 subcommittees and 5 task forces that focus on different issues.

Our subcommittees oversee a broad range of matters, from budget issues to diversity relationship managers who are responsible for working with their outside counsel on collaborative diversity efforts throughout the year. For example, the Leadership Development subcommittee is responsible for recommending leadership development and mentoring programs on an ongoing basis. One of our most industrious subcommittees is our Women's subcommittee, which provides a full range of programming throughout the year for the Division.

Q: How has your Diversity and Inclusion Committee grown over the past few years?

A: The LCDDIC which was founded in 2001 and initially consisted of 15 members, currently has over 170 members globally, many of whom have formal and/or informal leadership roles. The Committee's membership includes representatives from both the Legal and the Compliance departments, and representatives from both officer and non-officer levels within the Division. In addition, Human Resources and global Diversity and Inclusion personnel are active members of the Committee. The Committee has a rotating Chair who reports to the Division's Chief Operations Officer and consults directly with the Chief Legal Officer and LCD senior management on Committee initiatives. In addition, this year, a Vice-Chair position has also been established to further strengthen and support the level of firm engagement.

Initiatives are primarily fulfilled through 12 subcommittees and 5 task forces. This structure allows Committee members to be closely engaged in different initiatives that align with their specific interests. We believe that the current structure has played a significant role in the spike in participation and the increase of the Committee's sponsored programs and initiatives over the last decade.

Q: In what ways are the committee members involved?

A: In order to be a member of the Diversity and Inclusion Committee we require participation in our monthly meetings and active service on at least one of the subcommittees, primarily working on research, programming or awareness campaigns. We have a legion of people who have a strong commitment to continued improvement in strengthening our communities and making the workplace more diverse and inclusive.

Q: How are you able to drive that support?

A: One of the primary ways we drive support is the top-down support. We could not be as effective without the support and the leadership of our Chief Legal Officer, Eric Grossman, and the rest of the senior management team. Eric speaks on a regular basis not only about our firm's commitment, but also his efforts to maintain and have a meritocratic environment within the Legal Compliance Division and his personal commitment to diversity and inclusion. He is also accountable to our Chief Executive Officer, James Gorman. On an annual basis he reports to the CEO on our efforts. The fact that the commitment comes from the CEO, CLO and from the rest of senior

Continued

Insight: Diversity and Inclusion Are Business Imperatives *Continued*

management is very empowering and confirms that the efforts of the Committee members are aligned with the Firm's mission and supported by all.

Further, I often caution people who are establishing diversity committees or have some that don't work to look at their diversity committee: Is your diversity committee diverse, in every sense of the word?

Q. Is your committee global?

A: Yes, it is worldwide and we work with our colleagues in Europe and Asia to fulfull our initiatives globally.

Q: What would your advice be for diversity professionals?

A: A diversity professional's priority should always be obtaining top-down support. In order to be effective, you need to have the right relationships with the senior leadership within the organization. You must have their buy-in to help articulate the value proposition of the diversity inclusion mandate. Every firm is different, and so their core values, and how diversity can play a role, may vary. A diversity professional must be able to understand their firm's broader strategies and challenges to grasp how diversity can help solve issues or problems that senior management is facing every day.

What You Should Know

- Treat recruitment as a special part of your mission. It is.
- Get to know what it means to your organization. How do people get in as an entry or as an advanced professional? What is valued in the process? What are the proxies for success in the recruitment process? Grades, experience, types of prior organizational or industry experience, relationships?
- Know your external feeder institutions. Where do your new hires come from? Schools, law firms, companies? Any ones in particular? Do you know these people at these institutions? Is there a good relationship?
- Cultivate relationships with all possible sources, which means almost everyone in the industry, business, bar, etc. Anyone could be a hire. Always be on the hunt for good talent, whether you think you need it now or not.
- Expect to learn a lot with each hire. Apply those lessons with each subsequent hire. Whether it is more information about a school or prior organization, each hire will provide information about his or her prior experience and the hiring experience with your organization. Be curious and expect to learn valuable information.

CHAPTER 8

REACHING OUTSIDE THE ORGANIZATION

Or we are part of a larger but often smaller community!

Overview

The strategic focus of most diversity initiatives is centered on internal matters and the needs of the firm or organization. The driving force for establishing diversity and inclusion efforts is often the need to develop and advance the recruitment, retention, and promotion of a diverse workforce. Diversity goals for efforts outside the organization may not be included or even mentioned initially in the strategic plan, particularly if it is a relatively new initiative for the organization; however, such goals are essential to a comprehensive plan. To start, it is helpful to bifurcate your diversity and inclusion strategy to focus on both internal and external goals.

When developing an external strategy, the diversity professional must consider the following:

- Are the organization's external diversity and inclusion goals consistent with its internal goals?
- What contributions can the organization make?
- How will any contributions benefit the organization and the legal profession as a whole?
- Should one seek to establish partnerships with other organizations to advance these goals outside of the organization?
- Where do I start?

As a diversity professional, it is critical to stay abreast of diversity discussions and developments in the legal and business communities and determine how your organization can contribute. Developing relationships in the legal and business communities is key. This chapter will discuss how to develop an external diversity initiative and key diversity partnerships, including relationships with bar associations and nonprofit, community, and student organizations, as part of your strategic plan.

GETTING STARTED

To start, examine the diversity mission or goal statement to review stated diversity and inclusion goals. Mission statements and diversity goals should serve as living documents and should be updated and amended as the organization's initiative matures. Next, develop a plan (if a plan is in place, it may only need to be revised) to assist in implementing the external initiative. The external initiatives plan should take into consideration available resources and time and budgetary considerations. It is helpful to preidentify the types of partnerships that best fit the organizational needs and are within the constraints of organizational resources.

As an important resource to the organization, the diversity professional may be the face of the organization's initiative in the legal community. Keep in mind that the organization is part of the legal community, a community in which the need to advance diversity and inclusion is well-stated. Law firms and corporate legal departments have gone from passively supporting initiatives in the greater legal community to actively identifying and participating in such efforts. This contributes to building a legal profession that better reflects the many communities that the profession represents and serves to strengthen the legitimacy of the overall legal system and the confidence of the public. Of course, as a matter of equality, advancing a diverse and inclusive legal profession is the right thing to do and contributions from all sectors are essential in order to have a truly diverse and inclusive profession. From a business perspective, participating in external initiatives advances the organization's brand as an employer of choice and provides the opportunity to establish and strengthen existing relationships with nonprofit organizations, community organizations, corporations, and existing and potential clients.

Bar Associations

Bar associations are excellent resources. In many areas, bar associations have established specific goals focused on advancing diversity and inclusion in the legal profession. As part of such programs, bar associations have implemented initiatives to reach their stated goals, including diversity statements, which often require its signatories to aspire to reach certain stated objectives, including hiring and retention goals, the implementation of best practices, such as the hiring of a diversity professional (a recommended best practice), and the implementation of a diversity education and awareness programs. In addition to accessing bar association resources, participation on bar association diversity committees will offer the opportunity to assist in shaping the efforts of the committee, as well as being in the forefront of best practices, activities, and programs.

Minority bar associations are an excellent source of information and provide many partnership opportunities. At the national and local levels, minority bar associations have a specific focus and stated goals. For example, key partnerships at the national level may include the National Bar Association, National LGBT Bar Association, National Asian Pacific American Bar Association, and the Hispanic National Bar Association, to name a few. Local minority bar associations play an important role and offer the opportunity for local mentorship and important business and professional networking. Both are integral to the organizationn's strategic plan, but it is essential to identify how to best utilize such bar association relationships. For example, one can encourage individual membership among the attorney ranks (policies regarding organizational support for individual membership costs vary from organization to organization and should be considered), as well as support of the organization's fundraising activities and participation in programs and events. The diversity professional must examine the time, resources, and budget needs when evaluating how to best utilize your partnerships.

Nonprofit Legal-Related Organizations

Nonprofit organizations dedicated to advancing diversity in the legal profession are important partners and sources of information and innovation. There are many at both the local and national levels. Three of the most recognized national organizations that have a legal focus include the Minority Corporate Counsel Association, the Leadership Council on Legal Diversity, and the Institute for Inclusion in the Legal Profession. There are many well-established organizations, both at the local and national levels, and it is important to identify the focus areas of interest when learning about the organizations. Often these organizations offer membership opportunities and sponsor conferences and resources that may be available without membership or cost. In identifying partners, it is helpful to check the group's membership list. Look to see if peer organizations, well-known corporations, clients, or potential clients are members. Corporate partnership involvement also offers the opportunity for joint initiatives.

Community Organizations

Partnerships with community organizations are another effective way to advance diversity goals, including diversity pipeline efforts, and contribute significantly to local and national community efforts. There are literally hundreds of nonprofit community organizations that focus on building diversity from many perspectives. For example, elementary, middle, and high school programs can provide important outreach opportunities to assist children in underserved communities. There are programs that assist college students with law school prep, and legal-based organizations that seek to advance the civil and human rights of women, members of the LGBT community, and ethnic minorities. These can be important relationships and can fit in well with your external diversity initiatives. Such groups also may overlap with recruiting and retention initiatives as well as the organization's pro bono initiatives.

Pro Bono Service Organizations

A few words about working with the orgainzation's pro bono department or team. This relationship should be fluid, with good communication to advance the organization's joint diversity and pro bono goals. It is important to clarify that diversity initiatives should not be confused with pro bono efforts, but the goals may, and often do, overlap. Pro bono legal opportunities can reach and benefit many diverse communities. Working with the pro bono team, the diversity professional can implement strategies to develop opportunities for the lawyers to have greater outreach to diverse communities through the organization's pro bono efforts. For example, working with the NAACP Legal Defense and Education Fund, Asian American Legal Defense and Education Fund, Latino Justice, Lambda Legal, and other non-profit organizations can provide numerous opportunities for partnerships and advancement of pro bono and diversity efforts. Also, pro bono work is an excellent tool for the professional development of associates.

Clients and Corporations

Foremost among partnerships to include in the organization's external strategic plan are relationships with clients, potential clients, and other individuals and corporations. Diversity partnerships with existing clients can strengthen relationships to advance joint goals and can create potential business opportunities with organizations and individuals who are potential clients. Joint projects may take the form of community service projects, such as painting a school in an underserved community, teaming up for a breast cancer walk or run, or working together on a bar association committee, panel discussion, or legal matter. Collaboration, discussion, and communication are predicated on working together to advance joint diversity and inclusion goals.

Chevron's legal department demonstrates how it works closely with its advance joint diversity and inclusion goals.

Insight From an Industry Expert

Interview with Chevron's Law Function Diversity Council (LFDC) sponsor, Mary Francis, Chief Corporate Counsel, and chairperson, Josetta Jones, Supervising IP Counsel for the Downstream and Chemicals group

Chevron's legal department is one of the few departments that awards its law firms for their commitment to diversity within the legal profession. The LFDC evaluates its firms' employment of diverse and LGBT attorneys, the demographics of the attorneys that support Chevron matters, as well

Continued

Insight From an Industry Expert *Continued*

as the firms' external support of diversity and LGBT initiatives within the legal profession. When asked about their surveys that are sent to their law firms, they described their process, "...the law function publicly recognizes our outside counsel partners for their commitment to diversity. Around the beginning of the year, late first quarter or early second quarter, we'll send out a survey questionnaire asking our outside counsel,

- The number of diverse attorneys the firm has working on Chevron matters and in what practice areas? And how much are they are billing to Chevron matters.
- What does your diversity profile look like within your organization? Is it representative of a diverse organization of attorneys or is it less diverse?
- What types of programs does the firm support externally to advance diversity within the legal profession?
- Are you active in diverse bar associations, and are you recruiting diverse law students for your summer clerkship programs? What does that involvement and recruitment look like?

"After we have received from 30–50 responses, then the diversity council evaluates those responses and selects three law firm recipients to receive an award. And, I would say it's in this awards program and process, and not just sending a letter from our general counsel, that we recognize their efforts. We have a big ceremony and reception.... And, often we will have C-suite executives attend the ceremony and reception. In prior years, we have also had our CEO and chairman address the attendees about the importance of diversity and how it has impacted Chevron's legal matters"

When asked about their success with this effort, Chevron reports that they are seeing more diverse teams on their matters in a proactive manner where Chevron does not have to ask or suggest that the firms consider diversity in staffing. They also describe other benefits from their survey. "...Other successes are that people are becoming more comfortable with the dialogues about diversity rather than it being the elephant in the room. ...They [these firms] have dialogue with majority attorneys because really the diversity piece is about everybody. It's not really about one group, one ethnicity. It is about everybody; we all have to work together and so if we're able to open up this dialogue and have a more comfortable discussion....I think it can really resonate with our law function, our law department colleagues, not just the attorneys but also the staff. And I think with that discussion and recognition of diversity in the legal profession, we consider that a success."

Existing Organizational Systems

To be successful, the external initiative must be comprehensive, flexible, and consistent with how the organization operates. Look at existing systems to see if partnerships already exist, and then seek to expand or emphasize the diversity benefits that may already be taking place. If relationships do not exist, examine existing systems, such as affinity group programs or events, recruiting department goals, or associate development initiatives. Check with the marketing team and the person or committee who manages the organization's charitable contributions or corporate social responsibility team to ensure good communication and the ability to enhance efforts that are already taking place in order to further advance and emphasize the organization's external diversity goals. It is a good idea to take stock of this prior to or around the time to set budgetary needs, as it can help to clarify available resources for the next budgetary cycle as you look at short- and long-term planning.

What You Should Know

- Your organization is an integral part of the community. In some ways, you are an organizational neighbor. You must have some relationship with outside organizations. Be deliberate about the relationships. Understand the value of outside organizations and how they matter to your organization.
- As in any relationship, be as consistent as possible. If it is a sponsorship relationship, acknowledge that. If you want more, discuss it. If it will change, give notice.
- Always look for and be open to opportunities in the relationship. As circumstances, markets, and people change, relationships between organizations may need to be adjusted. Anticipate and maybe, sometimes, instigate adjustments, shifts, or changes in the relationships that can help sustain the relationship.

CHAPTER 9

PROFESSIONAL DEVELOPMENT AND RETENTION

Or the keys to success

Overview

Retaining a diverse workforce is one of the most important areas and functions of the diversity professional or team. It is the essence of success for the organization and answers the question of whether you are successfully recruiting and developing your human capital. A comprehensive and thoughtful infrastructure and framework must be in place to support the retention and advancement of all attorneys, in particular those who fall under the diversity umbrella. Professional development, collegiality, and inclusion are key elements of retaining employees. Retaining employees in a law firm or legal department requires an assessment of the opportunities for development, an understanding of the evaluative and promotional systems in place, and the development of programs and policies that monitor and track evaluations, professional development, and promotion/advancement on all levels. Concomitant with these efforts, a strong working relationship is needed with two key strategic partners: human resources and professional development. Integral to these relationships is a focus on attorney evaluations and professional development needs and opportunities.

To properly appreciate the challenges and opportunities of retention and professional development and the role of the diversity professional, it may be a useful exercise to conduct a basic assessment. Ask yourself, who is leaving and why? Who is staying and why? Who is being promoted and why? Continue this line of questioning and it will lead to a better appreciation of the tasks ahead.

As discussed in Chapter 14, data is a critical element in understanding the landscape of challenges and opportunities. This could not be more important than with respect to the data surrounding retention. Soliciting retention data can be a study in semantics. Often, employers track attrition, which is typically the employee turnover rate. This number will give you percentages of loss in your workforce, usually by category. This loss can be tracked by demographics, meaning you can determine if there is a higher rate of loss in particular groups. This is important data because it will give you a general perspective of the nature of employee turnover; however, this data will not reveal who is staying and who is leaving. To appreciate the retention element of this kind of data, it is necessary to track the organization's change in status reports on a regular basis.

Human resources typically maintains "change" reports. Usually provided on a weekly basis, this report tracks who is hired and who is terminated (a literal term that has no bearing on the nature of the departure, just who has left and will be "terminated" in the system). Working closely with the human resources department will ensure that diversity demographics data is included in this report, which allows for an appreciation of weekly changes in the workforce from a diversity perspective. Reviewing the change reports weekly, monthly, and yearly will allow sorting of this data by demographics, work sectors, location, and other factors, as well as changes among tenure groups (meaning determination of loss and retention by length of employment with firm/company). Assessing who remains is as important as who departs.

EXIT SURVEYS

The exit survey is an important assessment tool. Most human resources departments conduct exit surveys with departing employees. There is usually standard language in the questions. While there is some concern that this data may not yield the most candid responses, for varying reasons, it is still information that can be used, especially if that data is tracked for particular demographics. Again, a partnership with the human resources department can ensure that this information is captured and quantified into diversity demographics, as well as work sectors and tenure with the organization. While the human resources department may not sort or examine the data through a diversity lens, if the exit information is captured demographically, then crunching the data may provide invaluable information.

Often, the diversity professional has been consulted by the departed attorney, is aware of the reasons the person is leaving, and will know the "other" story, which is not always what is expressed in the exit survey. It is difficult to share this information, as it is not verifiable and usually inconsistent with what was expressed to human resources in the exit interview. One way to capture more candid information is to retain an outside consulting firm to conduct exit interviews. This can be an important tool in retention assessment and can provide verification of anecdotal data that has not been captured through the human resources department exit surveys. Over time, the external exit survey can serve as a point of comparison to the internal human resources exit data. This comparison can validate the human resources exit data over time.

Using an Outside Consultant for Exit Surveys

When using an outside consultant, there are some important factors to consider. First, the diversity professional must work closely with the human resources team and the consultant to develop an instrument that asks the questions needed to secure the information that is being sought. If at all possible, there should be a very close correlation between the questions asked in the internal exit survey and the outside consultant survey. This will allow the performance of a comparative analysis of the two. The methodology should provide anonymity to encourage the participant to be as candid as possible. However, in some cases, the sample size for a particular group or work sector may be so small that it will be impossible to provide data without revealing the participants. Be prepared to appreciate that some responses may not be dissected into work sectors if a particular group has had a limited number of departures. Also, a narrative script should be developed that will be used when the consultant calls the former employee. The script should begin with language that clearly identifies this effort as part of the diversity efforts of the employer. When the human resources department conducts its exit interviews, they should inform the departing employee that an outside consultant will be conducting an anonymous exit survey for the diversity team. This may help in getting a better response and also will explain why two surveys are being done.

Once a reasonable sampling of surveys to offer sufficient information as to why employees are *leaving* has been obtained, it is helpful to also determine why employees are *staying*. Consider a survey that goes beyond the typical "satisfaction" surveys that are currently used in the legal market. If an outside consultant was used to execute the exit survey, consider using the same consultant for a retention survey. This kind of survey involves direct communication with employees, providing an opportunity to capture more anecdotal comments than respondents may share in an online survey. The advantage of this kind of survey assessment is that the employer can identify specific programs and policies that employees value, while also learning about any areas that may be of concern to the current workforce.

ATTORNEY EVALUATIONS

To conduct a comprehensive assessment of attorney evaluations, a review of firm metrics is also important. As discussed in Chapter 14 on metrics, it is necessary to review the associate evaluation process and the promotion process metrics to determine if there are particular segments of the attorney workforce that are not successful in these processes. Ask the following questions:

- Are there any patterns, trends, or particular groups who are receiving the highest evaluations? Why?
- Are there any patterns, trends, or particular groups who are receiving the lowest evaluations? Why?
- If there are indications of promotions, what are the demographics of those who are on track for promotions?
- Who received bonuses and what are those demographics?

- Were there any unique issues raised in the evaluation process that may be specific to particular individuals? What are their demographics?
- What would a review of the demographics of the compensation metrics reveal?

Implicit in this review is an understanding of the evaluation and promotions process. The diversity professional should have intimate knowledge of the evaluation and promotions processes, including the details and results of the processes.

Evaluation Process

Every organization evaluates its employees. With attorneys, this process should involve both real-time assessments as well as periodic reviews. In the "time is money" world, there is often insufficient time to provide meaningful feedback, and sometimes the only substantive review or feedback comes during the review cycle. The feedback may not even come from the person who actually provided the review. It is critical for the diversity professional to understand the evaluation process. This understanding should include a critical eye toward how effective and efficient this process is for the person who is being evaluated. Before delving into the process, approach the study of this system with the following questions in mind:

- How often is the formal process?
- When does it begin with the new employee? Are there periodic and intermittent opportunities to review within the formal structure?
- Is there accessible and transparent information about the process?

With these questions in mind, the diversity professional can begin to know and understand the process.

What Is the Review Process?

Know the calendar cycle of the process. When does it begin? What is expected? Usually, most evaluative processes begin with a self-evaluation. This is typically followed by a collection of information from the supervising attorneys, who must submit some kind of evaluation in writing. It may be followed by interviews with the subject of the evaluation as well as the evaluators. After the evaluations are collected, what happens? What are the next steps? This kind of knowledge is essential to the development of programs that can assist in the demystification of the process.

Who Is Involved?

Is there an evaluation committee or department that focuses on reviews? Are there people who participate in the process at certain points? Is this information public? Who does what and at what intervals? Why are these people involved? Do they represent practice groups, divisions, offices, and so on? Is this group representative of the firm's demographics? Have they received any diversity education or training?

How Is the Information Collected?

There is usually a written process that involves input from the subject of the evaluation and the evaluators, but what happens then? Is it just a written evaluation process, or are interviews conducted? If interviews are included, who is involved in the interviews? How is the information recorded? Is there a master document that will include the written materials as well as a record of the interviews? Who creates that document?

Who Receives and Processes the Information?

After the information has been collected, who receives it? Is this information used as raw data or is a summary of the information? If there is a committee, does it review all the information? If not, who does? How is it decided what information is distributed to the committee? The sheer volume of the information may require some condensation. Is this the process? Is the information contained in a software program that provides access to the administrator or committee? The ultimate questions are, what information is presented to the committee, practice area, or administrator and how is this information compiled and presented?

How Are Decisions Made?

Who decides the ultimate evaluation that is delivered to the attorney? If it is an administrator system, does the decision rest in one person alone?

Who else may be a part of the process? Does the process have input before a final decision is made? Does anyone review the decision? In a committee or practice area system, what is the deliberative process? How is information presented to the committee or practice area as a whole? Do they meet in person? Do they review each attorney? Is there an advocate process that allows qualitative information to be presented? Is there a vote? Is there consensus? How are dissents handled?

What Are All Possible Outcomes?

Most evaluations do not have a "thumbs up" or "thumbs down" outcome. Usually, and depending on the tenure of the person being evaluated, there are many possible outcomes. It is crucial to understand all public and discreet outcomes. Are there qualitative ratings? Is there a ranking? Does it vary at different tenures? What impacts raises, merit, and/or discretionary bonuses?

Who Delivers the Information?

How does the recipient receive the information? Is there a written evaluation? Who writes it? Who reviews it? When is it delivered? Is there a delivery of any information in person? Is this the first time the recipient receives the information or is the meeting a review of information delivered in writing? If so, who is present? Who can be present? Can the person being reviewed bring his or her mentor or sponsor to the meeting where the information is delivered or reviewed?

What Are the Possible Responses and Is There an Appellate Process?

With most evaluative processes, the subject of the evaluation will have the opportunity to respond. How is this opportunity presented? If the subject does not agree with the evaluation, is there a formal process to revisit the decision? With whom would the attorney speak? What if there is no dispute with the substance of the evaluation, but the attorney is not happy with the compensation or bonus? Is there a process by which that decision can be revisited?

Knowledge of these answers will enable the diversity professional to have a comprehensive understanding of the process and provide educational programming to ensure that attorneys have sufficient information to manage the process.

PROMOTION PROCESS

The ideal retention model is one where the entering attorney develops, progresses, and is promoted, celebrated, and advanced. The promotion process is the obvious trajectory to success. What the process is and how it works is fundamental information that the diversity professional must master. This knowledge is also necessary for the attorney in the law firm and legal departments. It is the diversity professional's responsibility to understand this information and develop programs to inform and advance the process from a broader lens.

There are obvious roads to success in most law firms and legal departments. Whether success means ascension to the general counsel position or to an equity partnership, there are steps along the way and a process that guides those steps and determines progression. What are the steps of progression? What is the process for movement from one step to the next? What is required for each step? What is the decision-making process? Who is involved? How does one become a part of that process? How are decisions influenced? Who communicates the decision? These are important questions to answer in order to understand the process and how it is influenced. This information is vital for the success of the diversity professional in the area of retention. It is critical to have attorneys from diverse backgrounds master this process and have successful outcomes.

What Are the Steps of Progression?

First, understand the obvious steps of progression. Whether the employee is an assistant, associate, or lead counsel or an associate, senior associate, or partner, there are obvious steps and then there are the unpublished methods for successful completion of each step. Clearly, tenure and professional development are necessary elements. In understanding the steps of progression, know the expected tenure in each of the steps. How long does one typically invest in each step? What are the shortest and longest tenures? How are these steps defined formally and informally? Are there any unique processes involved in the progression of particular areas or groups?

What Is the Process for Movement from One Step to the Next?

How does one move along the path of progress? Is there a formal designation from one step to the next? How is the designation determined? Are there categories that are recognized as advancement? For example, "assistant" to "associate" connotes advancement. Progression to senior associate suggests a level of knowledge and seniority. Sometimes, there is a designation of a certain number of years of experience for partnership consideration. How is that designation applied and when does it happen?

What Is Required for Each Step?

What competencies are attached to each step? How does one access those competencies in each of the areas in the institution? Is there an expected level of competency to advance through each step? What are the competencies required for each area? Are they made clear to employees? How available are the opportunities to acquire those competencies? How is competency measured and evaluated from step to step?

What Is the Decision-Making Process?

How are the decisions to advance someone made? Are materials collected? Who contributes? What are the materials? How are they collected? Are there interviews? How are they recorded? Who synthesizes interviews? Who reviews the materials? What is the decision-making model? Are the decision makers a group, and what is the decision process? Does there need to be consensus? Is there a review process, and who is that group? Is there an appellate process before the decision is communicated?

Who Is Involved?

Who is involved in the decision-making process? If it is a committee, what is the membership criterion and how does one become a member? If it is less than a committee, on whose authority does the group or individual operate? To whom do they report? Is there an approval process before decisions are final? Who is involved in that process? Are there key leaders who must provide formal or informal approval before a decision is made? Is a section head required to support the nomination? Is the support of a practice group leader required?

How Are Decisions Influenced?

What are the most important factors in getting promoted at the institution? There are usually published criteria and then there is informal information that is known to be essential. What is that information? Is it a standard of performance and experience (e.g., sitting first chair in litigation areas, independent management of deals in transaction, meeting quantifiable goals such as hours or supervision, etc.)? Are there key players whose opinion is required before a final decision is made? Is that an informal or formal requirement? Does anyone have a tipping point where they can persuade the decision? Is there information that can affect the decision? Does it matter how many people are in the class being considered for promotion? Does group or section matter? It is imperative to know how decisions are influenced, as this may have a significant impact on a particular class of promotions or individuals. It is crucial that the diversity professional stay aware of these influencers and how they impact the diversity community.

Who Communicates the Decisions?

How does one learn of a promotion? Who communicates the good or unexpected information is important. Is it a formal process or is that decision made informally? Does it matter if the decision is not favorable? Is the diversity professional involved in the communications?

The answers to these questions are equivalent to an informal assessment. This data is important for the diversity professional's success in this area. The diversity professional must have a working knowledge of the status of retention matters, appreciate the opportunities and needs, and determine the menu of programming that can educate and support efforts and goals. The challenges and opportunities presented by the answers to the above questions will suggest the kinds of education and programming needed. An understanding of the processes and influencers will guide the substance and sophistication of the programming as well as priority setting. It is important to be responsive and proactive in this vital area. A careful analysis of the data obtained from the questions and the qualitative understandings will suggest ways to establish goals and develop programs. It is important to be strategic about education and programming, as there are many opportunities to be responsive and proactive to advance retention goals. How you define your greatest opportunities and needs will frame the goals that may be developed. Designing programs specific to those goals will be strategically sound and tactically relevant. There are some important considerations when exploring the programmatic aspect of this area. For purposes of this discussion, it is helpful to examine programs for the evaluation and promotions processes.

Attorney Development Programming

Attorney development programs are designed primarily to supplement and support the learning and development of the attorney. This should include practice area–specific training, identified competencies for stage development, specific training attached to competencies, and mentoring and coaching. Outreach to and inclusion of the professional development team and diversity professional are important and helpful to advance strategic diversity and inclusion, attorney development, and retention goals. Such programming does not differ in substance, but the delivery, timing, structure, and offerings may vary in order to focus the lens on diversity and experiences. There may be more detailed sessions offering specificity on particular aspects of the subject area: for example, programming may include mentoring across differences (e.g., cultural, generational, economic) or doing business globally. Whatever the specific topic, working together the professional development team can provide proactive programming for the entire firm for the evaluation, promotion, and advancement process.

The diversity professional should be aware of the menu of services available under the professional development umbrella. There should be room for collaboration at the intersections of programming and budget. While the diversity team may not have professional development programming in their budget, it's important for the diversity team to make the professional development group and the evaluations and the compensation committees aware of the organization's diversity objectives. Members of the professional development team should be invited, included, and encouraged to participate in diversity programs, as it is key to have as many stakeholders as possible involved in supporting compliance, advocacy, and success.

Professional development programming can be adopted by affinity groups presenting CLE programs on substantive areas (usually teams with client invitations for business development), coaching and coaches specific to individual affinity groups, and seminars at affinity retreats (time management, stress management, etc.). It is important to appreciate all opportunities to educate and enlist the support of other departments and key firm and diversity leaders to develop the programs and policies.

Intersecting with the Professional Development and Attorney Development Teams

The diversity professional should ask the following questions:

- Are there stated competencies for the trajectory of the attorney?
- Are there stated competencies for each practice area?
- Are they published and easily accessible?
- Is advancement predicated upon completion and proficiency in competencies?
- Is there training available for all of the competencies?
- Is it readily available and accessible?
- Is there a formal mentoring program?
- How is diversity valued in the programming, selection and evaluation of the mentor program?
- Is there any collection of demographic specific data for measuring effectiveness of professional development programming?
- Are there coaching services available?
- Are the coaches from diverse backgrounds?
- How is diversity valued in the coaching programs?
- How can the diversity professional be of value to the professional development team?
- Is there programming for any of the above?

Evaluation Programming

Programming around the systemic function of evaluations should be responsive and proactive to the needs and opportunities presented. Needs are determined through a study of the assessments and data received. This assessment will reveal what the population needs to understand. It will disclose what education needs to be provided and who needs it, when, and how. The opportunities presented are the pragmatic, efficient, and realistic avenues to address the needs identified and prioritized by goal setting. There will be opportunities to provide more education around the processes. There could be a need to provide more specificity with samples and models and an opportunity to provide training to the key players and decision makers. There is always an opportunity to monitor and track the success and development of the attorneys involved. Programming can run the gamut, and the diversity professional should lead and facilitate the programming in a way that is responsive, proactive, and consistent with the strategic diversity and inclusion goals that have been identified.

Programs Focused on the Attorney Evaluation Process

Types of programs that can be developed in the area of evaluations include:

- Educational programming that defines the evaluation processes—this may include seminars, webinars, or online information about the formal processes. This program or data would give a timetable and dates with specific information about the mechanics of the process. This information is typically offered or reinforced at new employee or associate retreats.
- Affinity groups can focus on specific programming that includes greater detail. This may include participation from human resources, specific information on what is expected in personal statements, interviews, etc. Such programming may also provide sample personal statements, tips on interviews, or tips on navigating the hiring process. This more detailed type of program may also include solicited and/or staged questions around key

Continued

Programs Focused on the Attorney Evaluation Process *Continued*

areas and nuances.

- Diversity awareness training with a focus on evaluative processes, including recognizing and avoiding unintentional bias, that can be offered to all members of the evaluation committee or others involved in the process. This tailored training program can focus on systemic issues that may have an unintended impact on different segments of the organization. It may also serve as a team-building experience by developing shared experience while learning to understand and appreciate that diversity education is important and integral to evaluative systems.
- Programs designed to increase the participation of evaluators in the process. Many organizations have goals to increase the number of persons evaluating attorneys, thereby ensuring that the person being evaluated has the benefit of feedback from all those who have given assignments.
- Programs that instruct attorneys or associates to solicit or give real-time feedback. These programs can be designed to instruct the attorney to solicit feedback in a timelier manner than the formal process. The best learning and professional development happens in an environment conducive to interaction between the supervising attorney and the other attorneys. Soliciting feedback through face-to-face interaction or by using resources that provide feedback on the work product is a critical element in the learning process and is very valuable.

Programs Focused on Attorney Advancement

Types of programs that can be developed in this area include:

- Forums that provide detailed and supplemental information designed for and by affinity groups. Whether at a retreat or as a standalone program, forums can provide tips on the process and examples of excellence for written materials, as well as present insights into nuances and unpublished perspectives on the process.
- Diversity awareness programs with a focus on the promotions process, which can be very helpful in educating the members of the evaluation team and practice area leaders. This is a tailored training that focuses on any systemic issues identified that may have an unintended impact on the different segments of the organization. This program may also serve as a team-building experience, developing a shared experience for the evaluative group.
- Attorney monitoring programs with an emphasis on the importance of tracking hours as well as the sophistication of projects and supervision. These programs may also include an analysis of the importance of external relations leadership experience.
- Programs that support lateral integration, which can articulate expected deliverables and timetables. There may also be policy considerations that could extend the timetable for achieving the stated goals.

What You Should Know

Professional development is an essential element in the retention of employees, particularly lawyers. People stay because they learn and grow, but also because they feel they are making a contribution that is valued and appreciated. The diversity efforts should be involved in the planning and implementation of the attorney-development experience, including the evaluation process.

CHAPTER 10

AFFINITY/EMPLOYEE RESOURCE GROUPS

Or group benefits

Overview

Effectively managed, employee resource or affinity group programs are an excellent resource and complement diversity and inclusion strategies and initiatives. Employee resource groups impact law firms and legal departments in three significant areas: recruitment, retention and promotion, and lawyer satisfaction. In addition, the groups serve as a platform and offer direct access to like networks at law schools and corporations. Although frequently referred to as "affinity groups," there is a growing trend to identify the groups as "employee resource groups" or "inclusion networks." This change reflects the increasing focus on aligning group objectives and goals with the business purpose of the organization, and clarifying and heightening the focus of the groups as being inclusive. The groups serve as valuable professional resources to their members and the organization, rather than being a social group.

A frequent criticism of implementing organizationally sanctioned affinity groups is that they may be perceived as divisive—and why would an organization want to implement an initiative that appears to encompass the exact opposite of what it is trying to achieve? To answer this, it is critical to understand the "business case" or rationale for building and advancing this initiative, the benefits to group members and effective group structure and organization. Organized strategically, the groups add value to the organization's inclusion efforts. This chapter will discuss the business case for affinity groups, group benefits to the firm and members, group structure options, and getting the most from the group. A brief discussion regarding religious and political groups and networks is included.

The Business Case

For many organizations, affinity groups existed informally or at a grassroots level prior to being formalized by the organization. The groups and networks serve as a source of information and support for group members, who are typically statistically underrepresented in the organization. Although early affinity group programs focused primarily on women, ethnic minorities, and openly LGBT lawyers, the groups have expanded to include persons with disabilities, women of color, parents, veterans, members from select geographic regions, multicultural groups, and others.

Diversity recruiting is an important aspect of any law firm and legal department diversity strategy and a recognizable benefit of affinity groups. Law school affinity groups, such as Black, Asian, Hispanic, LGBT, women, and others, are well-developed in law school culture and have grown in popularity and importance. A prime benefit of law firm affinity groups is to link with student groups for direct recruiting access and communication. This level of access is also helpful in terms of positive on-campus branding via the organization's inclusion network interactions with like law school groups (which cannot be replicated by the organization as a whole) and the opportunity to garner greater understanding of student perspectives and concerns. Law firm or legal department interaction can often take the form of participation in law school group programs and informal mentoring.

At the other end of the spectrum, law firm affinity groups are also a natural link to corporate employee resource groups. They can offer firms unique opportunities to interact with corporations, clients, and potential clients for the purpose of advancing joint organizational diversity and inclusion goals and advancing business opportunities. It is important for the diversity professional to be cognizant of this platform and the opportunity for group members to improve and expand their professional networks, mentor informally and formally, and take part in professional development and networking as part of the affinity network initiative.

Group Benefits to Organization and Members

In addition to network building outside of the organization, affinity groups promote retention and promotion through opportunities to mentor informally and cross-market professional skills within the organization and network. This is particularly true for groups that work together on outreach and pipeline initiatives in diverse communities. These and other such projects engage group members beyond their regular client work and create individual connections to the group, colleagues, and projects in and outside of the organization. Further, group members typically have the opportunity to interact with senior members of the organization who are participating. Affinity groups can enhance and promote a positive organization brand, serving as an extension of the organization's commitment to diversity and inclusion both inside and outside the organization. This can significantly impact recruiting and client marketing efforts and it assists in building internal relationships, which are critical to retention and promotion efforts. *One of the most significant benefits this initiative can offer to the organization is attorney satisfaction.* Group participation creates a stakeholder interest in the organization, connecting lawyers/staff with the organization beyond client work, and helps to reduce early and unexpected attrition. Participation in group decisions, activities, and programs also offers prospects for leadership, organizational development, and other skills where the opportunity for development may not be as readily available.

Where to Start: Strategic Planning

Employee resource groups must be purposeful and focused—consider the following questions:

- What are the overall goals of the network initiative?
- Are there any limitations to group formation?

- Who can be a group member? Attorneys? Staff?
- How will membership be determined?
- Who can participate in activities?
- How will group success be measured?
- How will the groups be supervised?
- How will group resources be determined?

The diversity professional should assist group members in developing a mission statement or similar method for determining group goals. These goals should be aligned with, and advance, the goals of the organization as well as the members. *A word about being exclusive: It is a better practice to include all who wish to participate in advancing the group's mission, rather than limit group membership to only those members who possess the certain attributes that the group focuses on, such as race, gender, or LGBT status.* Allies are necessary to the advancement and mission of all groups and the organization's overall diversity goals. All members who commit to advancing such goals are an important resource for the group.

Critical to group success is a commitment from organizational leaders and senior sponsorship. Whether through membership or in an advisory capacity, senior level participation is necessary to link group goals to senior leaders and to establish a line of communication with the organization's leadership. As a practical matter, this can be extremely important in terms of resource allocation, budgets, and organizational significance. It also reflects the value the organization places on the groups and the benefits of advancing organizational goals.

Next, the quid pro quo. As mentioned above, the members must benefit, but so must the organization. This can be done simply by looking for group alignments, such as recruiting and client and professional development. For example, if an inclusion network is focused on recruiting efforts, then such effort should be aligned with the organization's recruiting department so that the efforts of group members can be organized and function as a true resource. This is an indispensable benefit for the organization and the group.

Group Structure

There are many ways to structure affinity group networks, but a great deal of consideration must be given to making sure the groups fit well within the organization's culture and are not inadvertently outside of current federal and state employment laws. Current best practices include making the groups voluntary, in terms of both group existence and membership. Predetermined groups organized by the organization's diversity professional, human resource group, or other department can be helpful in certain cultures and meet group needs; however, it can also lessen individual involvement and group momentum. In addition to formation, membership must be considered. As noted above, often a senior member of the organization will be connected to the group to serve as a liaison to senior management and demonstrate the importance of the group to the organization—this is an important statement for current and potential group members. Depending on group needs, however, senior level membership can have a chilling effect on the ability of the more junior members to have candid discussions and develop ideas. In such cases, it is important to address this concern and establish group dynamics that promote candid discussion. Senior participation also may be in the form of advisors to assist the group in navigating within the organization and serving as a link to senior management. Keep in mind that whatever structure is implemented, it must be in line with the culture of the firm. If it is inconsistent and completely outside of how the organization functions, it is less likely to be successful, which can be detrimental to other retention tools.

A positive way to demonstrate and develop group inclusion is to encourage group membership to all who wish to participate, rather than limit membership to specific group attributes, for example allowing only women to join the women's group. The diversity professional should emphasize the mission and goals of the group, rather than the limitations on membership. With that said, however, the decision should be made with the input of group members. It is important to note that there are many cases in which organizations limit membership to lawyers only, as it may be determined that there is a greater need to focus on advancing attorney recruitment, retention, and promotion strategies. It is critical to first look at the culture of the organization and even the specific office to make sure such a strategy fits well within the culture. As full inclusion must be the ultimate goal in any diversity strategy, a plan should be developed to include full participation as a goal of the group.

Group leadership must be identified, and should be voluntary and limited to a specific time period to avoid leadership burnout, which is not uncommon if the time frame is not well-defined and the same group of participants is relied upon to participate. Leadership rotation, whether through assignment or a voting process, encourages the opportunity for leadership development and new member participation. It is often easier to do your best and give 100 percent if you know that the responsibility will end at a specific time. There are many benefits to serving as a group leader, including opportunities to develop leadership skills, increase exposure within the organization, and represent the group outside of the firm. However, it is important that the experience not detract from the person's goal of providing excellent legal service. Be careful that the attorney is not informally viewed as a full-time affinity group leader, which will certainly detract from the primary goal of the individual and the group: advancing retention and promotion.

Group focus is critical. This can be accomplished through the mission statement or statement of goals, which will focus the group, potential group members, and the firm on the function and direction of the group. The group leadership and members should develop the statement, with input and review by the diversity committee and/or senior management so that the expectations are clear to all and consistent with broader organizational goals. The statement of goals should include the organization's expected benefits from the group, that is, the quid pro quo—for example, group participation in recruiting events and summer associate programs and serving as an advisor with respect to certain firm-requested external sponsorship.

Groups should determine annually or semi-annually the types of programs and initiatives that they would like to implement so there can be ample planning time and budget consideration. Working with the organization's calendar is important so that group efforts do not duplicate other events. Budgets will inevitably vary based on many factors, including group objectives; however, there is much groups can do that do not cost much and do not require a reinvention of the wheel. For example, diversity recruiting events should include affinity group participation, professional development, and training programs. They may also include programs cosponsored by affinity groups or joint pro bono and affinity group projects that support community outreach, such as affinity groups aligned with the firm's external sponsorship opportunities. The implementation of a speaker series could focus on relevant speakers known to members of the organization and who do not charge a speaker's fee. It is critical to examine existing systems, events, and projects to see where there are possible alignments and synergies for affinity group participation. This may also include partner or attorney retreats.

Getting the Most from the Group

Assisting the groups in developing and implementing their missions will offer members a tremendous opportunity for professional development, networking, a real connection to the organization, and workplace satisfaction. These groups are a valuable asset in advancing many diversity goals within the organization and should be one of the hallmarks of the organization's diversity and inclusion strategy. If the groups are led by senior level partners or attorneys within the organization who may not otherwise have an affinity to the group, it can be a positive experience as it will offer a firsthand account and direct insight into the experiences, issues, and concerns advanced by the group's mission and expected goals. Such leadership can also help to build more champions for the group within the organization. This is also true if the partners or senior leaders are not leading the efforts, but serve as advisors to the group. The experience gained in reaching a deeper understanding and developing individual relationships is great and extremely worthwhile.

PROGRAMMING

As discussed in Chapter 9, affinity group programming can take many forms; typically it is very broad and diverse. A good way to determine the types of programs that may be best for a particular group is to look at the group's mission statement or stated goals. Although there are many worthy programs to participate in, host, sponsor, and attend; time and resources are usually limited, given that members have primary responsibilities as practitioners and stakeholders of the organization. Starting with programs that can be linked to achieving the group's goals is a good benchmark and will help members to sort through the group's many options. For example, if a group goal is to support and advance the professional development of group members, then a group-specific skills development program focused on the "how to" for group members may advance that goal. Community outreach and partnerships with nonprofits, bar associations, and corporations may also be aligned with group goals. Programming that achieves more than one group goal, such as recruiting and professional development, is very desirable as it increases the group's return on its investment.

Programming can be very broad and diverse; in addition to hosting or sponsoring skills programs, other types of programming can be professionally beneficial and rewarding, for example education on substantive areas of the law, various management and leadership skills development, community outreach to diverse communities, pipeline programs, alumni outreach, or partnerships with law schools, nonprofits, bar associations, clients, and corporations. Group retreats are also an important aspect of affinity groups and can enhance group interaction and performance in significant ways. This is discussed more fully in Chapter 13 on retreats. Getting to know group members individually and their respective professional expertise/areas of practice is important—both in terms of developing relationships and the opportunity to market and share professional services—a critical element for business development.

Toolkits that function as "how-to" guides are excellent resources for inclusion networks. They enable group members to effectively organize and execute programs and events without reinventing the wheel each time. Such resources improve efficiency and reduce the frustration and stress that can often accompany program and event management responsibilities. Often, toolkits are developed for group retreats and other annual or recurring events.

Promoting group activities through events and programs advances important goals, including the primary goal of diversity retention. Such activities encourage and permit group members to function outside of their primary practice roles, build leadership and management skills, and develop ownership with and connect to the firm on multiple levels—all of which contributes to improved workplace satisfaction. One concern with programming is the need to continuously find creative and innovative topics and opportunities. Communication with group members can be helpful in this respect; for example, use a quick online survey, such as Survey Monkey, to identify timely areas of discussion and ideas.

Religious and Political Groups

The implementation of religiously based affinity groups continues to grow and add value to organizations. It is important to keep in mind when discussing the business case for such groups that there may be perceived challenges in connection with the organization of religious networks. Court cases, such as *Moranski vs. General Motors Corporation*, 433 F.3d 537 (2005), have helped define the framework and basic rules with regard to implementing religious inclusion network programs. It may be helpful to consult with the organization's employment attorneys for guidance in this area. Religious groups often advance the diversity goal of inclusion by furthering awareness of religious and cultural practices and giving group members a better sense of organizational inclusion.

Political groups, such as the Young Democrats or Young Republicans, may present challenges, in large part because the definition of what constitutes a political group may be broad and can open the door to groups whose mission and advocacy may not be well-aligned with the overall business objectives of the organization. Organizations may exclude religious and political affinity groups entirely from their approved networks to avoid concerns of discrimination or possible litigation. However, such groups have sometimes been approved with well-crafted criteria, including how they will benefit the organization and the members and advance the organization's diversity goals and overall business objectives.

What You Should Know

Appreciate that affinity/employee resource groups are an important retention tool within the organization.

- Recognize and understand the will of the group members as to its mission and goals. Listen to what is important to the group and encourage them to be consistent with the organization and department's mission.
- Support the exploration of success for the group. Provide leadership on annual goals and annual evaluations. Work to insure that they have set goals, activities and evaluations of such goals and activities.
- Focus on the leadership development of the groups. Also, pay attention to leadership succession to ensure continuity. Educate the affinity group leaders on budget projections, concerns, and accountability.

CHAPTER 11

DIVERSITY PROGRAM PLANNING

Or how to get it done

Overview

Programs are effective tools in diversity work. Described as "a planned series of events, items, or performances," programs are the panels, dinners, CLEs, conferences—the activities that support the implementation of strategies and tactics. It is important to understand and appreciate the role that programs play in the big picture. Defining and understanding the purpose of programs is required to appreciate how that program advances the effort and is effective. Always ask why the program is needed. What does it provide that is effective? How does the program support the larger vision and the overall goals?

Once it is understood how and why the program is necessary and effective, the approach and mechanics can be formulaic. In this chapter, we will discuss how to evaluate whether the program is necessary and effective. Ideally, the diversity professional should invest significant time in strategically planning and evaluating the program. Planning the event can be managed in a way that allows maximum time for strategic development. To that end, this chapter will also provide a basic guide to the mechanics of fundamental programming.

Getting Started with the Program

In addition to supporting the overall mission of the diversity efforts, programs should educate, develop, encourage, connect, and inspire. The questions that should follow each of those verbs are who, what, and why.

Educate whom, teach what, educate why? Develop whom, what, and why? Answering these questions and assigning the program in these kinds of categories facilitates the understanding of how the program contributes to or advances diversity efforts. If the answers to these questions lead to your mission, strategy, and goals, then the program is necessary and effective.

Consider this example: The members of an affinity group have presented a proposal for a firm-wide retreat. It is their position that a retreat will provide necessary fellowship, as the attorneys are divided into very small groups across many offices. The attorneys feel isolated and disconnected from others in the firm. The firm and the diversity committee have identified retention and professional development as priorities.

The diversity professional must connect the needs identified with the priorities established. A retreat is a program. How can this retreat advance the goals and priorities of the diversity efforts? Structure the retreat to include panels that educate the attorneys about the firm's systems, such as the evaluation and compensation systems. Other panels should provide information that can support the development of professional skills or connections, such as meeting by practice group or having senior associates provide insight into success. Offer opportunities for the attorneys to discuss their concerns, ideas, and suggestions. Provide opportunities for the attorneys to network with each other and invited firm leaders. A retreat that offers these opportunities is a program that is necessary and effective because it meets the goals of the diversity committee and the attorneys, which include retention and professional development. The analysis of this example can be extrapolated to any program. It is always helpful to have and perform a checklist when evaluating a program. For further discussion, see Chapter 13 on retreats.

Program Checklist

- Review the department or firm's diversity goals or priorities
- Ask the following questions:
  - Why are you presenting the program?
  - Does this program advance diversity efforts?
  - How does this program support the priorities or goals?
  - What function does it serve (educate, develop, connect, inspire, encourage)?
  - Is it worth the investment of time and energy as opposed to an investment in something that is more closely connected to the priorities and goals?
  - If not, what function does it serve and how does it merit time and attention?

Remember that most programs will meet one of the key functions. *Sometimes, a program does not meet the goals or priorities, but it meets a need that is worth the time and effort.* This could be an affinity program that does encourage and connect, but does not advance the formal goals, although it is important to validate the needs of the group. There will be many programs that will meet many goals. The key is to ensure that your diversity efforts are strategic and thus that the programs have strategic goals. Programs without strategic goals are akin to smoke and mirrors, with the appearance and investment of a lot of work, but their magic is short-lived and does not move the needle. Know why you are doing the program and how it advances your diversity journey. Below is a quick guide to the functions and goals of various programs.

Functions of Programs

Educate: Provide information
Develop: Target professional skills or requirements
Connect: Bring folks together, expose them to networks
Inspire and Encourage: Validate, reinvigorate, rally the troops

SAMPLE TOOLKIT

Following is a sample toolkit to assist in preparing for a diversity program:

Quarterly Roundtable

This is a quarterly event designed to allow the entire office an opportunity to have meaningful conversations about diversity (e.g., generational, racial, gender, etc.) in an informal setting. It usually takes place in the largest conference room during lunch time, with food available. Staff is encouraged to attend. This program presents an opportunity to provide formal education on a current topic or allow a casual but facilitated discussion on a specific aspect of diversity.

This is an event in X office. Topics have included generational, racial, gender, and LGBT diversity, as well as issues relating to substance abuse, anxiety, and depression. The event is hosted in-house, but has also included a movie night at a local theater and a follow-up discussion the next day during the quarterly roundtable.

Recommendations for the Planning Committee

The planning committee should have a minimum of two (2) members, consisting of at least one member of the Diversity Committee and someone in administration. Adequate staffing is critical to the event's success. At least one (1) committee member and one (1) or two (2) office volunteers are needed on the day of the event to oversee logistical and administrative issues, to handle last-minute problems, and to greet guest speakers and assist with their needs/concerns.

Budget

The total budget for this event may range from $2000 to $2500, for example. This amount includes fees paid to guest speakers and the cost of providing food for attendees.

Logistics

The committee's organization of the event will make it a success. That means securing a location, inviting guest speakers, sending out reminder e-mails, and selecting a menu, among other things. Recommendations include selecting a topic and reaching out to potential speakers and sending talking points and event programs to speakers.

Marketing and Promotion

This event requires minimal pre-event marketing and promotion. However, having diversity signage on hand and a digital camera to take pictures for internal marketing.

Day of Event

On the day of the event, at least one (1) committee member and one (1) or two (2) office volunteers should be on hand to finalize logistical concerns, handle last-minute issues, greet attendees, and take photos.

Post-Event Debriefing

It is important to have a meeting with the committee to debrief. Feedback—both positive and negative—will ensure successful events in the future.

Timeline

One month prior: Select a date and topic. Decide on guest speakers. Extend an invitation to speakers and confirm their attendance.

Two weeks prior: Reserve a conference room. Send e-mail invitation to office. Select a menu. Contact office services to discuss room setup, audio/visual needs, beverage service, and janitorial needs.

One week prior: Send follow-up e-mail confirming the attendance of those who have RSVP'd. Finalize catering order and submit check request.

Submit check requests for speaker fees. Send confirmed speakers talking points and event program. Reserve firm's digital camera.

Day of event: Send reminder e-mail to office. Confirm room is set up and beverage service is in place. Confirm food set up. Greet speakers and escort them to event site.

Logistics Checklist

- Invite speakers and confirm attendance
- Reserve room
- Send out e-mail invitation to office
- Select a menu
- Contact office services to discuss room set up, beverage service, audio/visual needs and maintenance and janitorial services
- Send reminder e-mail to office
- Finalize catering order
- Submit check request for speaker fees and lunch
- Send confirmed speakers talking points and event program

Marketing and Promotion Checklist

- Display diversity signage
- Bring digital camera to take pictures

Day of Checklist

- Send reminder e-mail to office
- Confirm food and room set up
- Bring digital camera

Wrap-Up and Evaluation Checklist

- Schedule a meeting no more than two weeks after the event
- Complete a brief survey or evaluation
- Compile a folder for suggestions for next year
- Store all relevant event documents in binder (e.g., sample invitations, invoices, thank you notes, etc.)
- Draft thank you e-mail
- Post photos and quotes from event on organization's internal website

Quarterly Roundtable Discussions Budget

Food for four events $2,000.00
Miscellaneous $500.00
TOTAL $2,500.00

Diversity roundtable invitations go out via a calendar invitation to the entire office. Below is an example of text included for one of the lunches.

Sample Text

Our next Diversity Roundtable lunch discussion is scheduled for **Wednesday, April 15**. This quarter, we will be discussing disability in the workplace. Once again, we will have a panel of speakers, including Jane Doe and Steve Blank (from the Detroit offices) and Bob Jones (adjunct professor at ABC Law School). Please accept this invitation if you are planning to attend. This lunch is sponsored by the Detroit Diversity Committee. It is optional and not compensable for overtime purposes. We look forward to your participation.

What You Should Know

- Programs are the meat and potatoes of any diversity initiative. They are the education and implementation of the efforts. Programs must be managed in an excellent and efficient manner. Access and involvement should be effortless and easy with a culture of invitation and inclusion.
- Remember to establish some regular programming that will be easy to develop and maintain. Then your sophisticated programming can focus on more sophisticated goals that advance the mission.

CHAPTER 12

CONSULTANTS AND SPEAKERS

Or how to maximize your return on investment from paid experts

Overview

Diversity professionals will need to rely on the resources of professionals outside the organization. These resources are available in all areas and the challenge is to identify the best professional for your organization and needs. It is also crucial to maximize the experience through engagement, partnership, and understanding of the value added. The diversity professional must engage the consultant or speaker in a manner that provides sufficient evaluative data. Upon selection, create a partnership in order to develop a deliverable that meets all expectations within the organization. Through this process, a relationship should develop that provides opportunities to explore and create new products, approaches, and deliverables that add value to your organization.

Selecting a consultant or a speaker can be a scary proposition. A great choice can make a huge contribution and a disappointing choice can require precious time spent in explanations, or worse, damage control. Regardless of the subject, need, or audience, here are some fundamental rules for selecting a consultant or speaker:

- **Do not hire anyone you have not seen in action.** If that is not possible, then credible recommendations must be vetted extensively.
- **Solicit as many reviews as possible.** Try to get reviews from sources who have a similar organizational style, values, size, and so on.

- **Review the website.** Know all that the speaker or consultant offers. Learn about their history, background, activities, successes, and involvements. This information gives context and depth to their potential understanding of your organization and why their services are needed.
- **Conduct at least two interviews.** The first interview should identify the need for the professional consultant. How the consultant will be utilized should be discussed, as well as your specific needs, goals, concerns, deliverables, and protocols. The second interview should be centered on the professional's proposal in response to the first interview.
- **Schedule at least two more opportunities to connect with the consultant before the event.** If there is an opportunity to observe the consultant or speaker before your event, try to arrange it.
- **Discuss specific protocols.** This could include confidentiality statements, travel arrangements, expectations of arrival and participation in other events, cost and payment, and so on.

Consultants provide many benefits, the most obvious being their objectivity and expertise. However, most organizations invest in many professional positions and have extensive internal resources. Hiring an outside consultant should not be a casual decision; it is important to be confident that this is a necessary expenditure. Before you hire a consultant, it is important to develop and review a checklist.

Consultant Checklist

- Why do you need a consultant?
- How do you identify a consultant?
- How do you select a consultant?
- How do you get the most out of a consultant?
- How do you get the best out of a consultant?
- Could there be mutual development?

Why Do You Need a Consultant?

The consultant or speaker should meet a need that cannot be met internally. The reasons for this should be obvious. Within the diversity construct, what is the need? If it is a consultant, is the purpose part of the long-term strategy, goals, and/or vision? Is the benefit obvious? Is there a specific deliverable that is clear, with critical buy-in? Does the hiring of this consultant meet a specific goal, and where is that goal on the list of priorities? If the consultant is a speaker, then who is the audience and what is the message? Will the audience understand the message? Is the audience expecting the message? Does this meet a communications need? Also, do not forget to identify smaller group presentations with more strategic groups that may not require a big presentation or project.

How Do You Identify a Consultant?

Aside from the internet and professional services organizations, word of mouth from colleagues is one of the best and most reliable ways to identify a professional consultant. Attending conferences and hearing these professionals speak is also a helpful way to identify a professional. Sometimes, there are panelists who are not necessarily speakers or consultants but may be able to serve a purpose for your organization. It may not always be a professional relationship where fees are exchanged. Sometimes, a colleague or expert in another area may be a resource. Travel and expenses may be inducement enough to bring someone in to speak with executives, lawyers, leaders, or departments.

How Do You Select a Consultant?

It can be difficult to select a consultant or speaker who meets your needs. There are several variables that must be considered, most of which are subjective, although some are objective. Consider the following variables:

- Do you like the person? Do they inspire confidence and respect?
- Do they have mass appeal? Are they relatable? Can they communicate effectively, particularly for your organization?

- Do they present well? Are they organized? Are they responsive? Are they attentive? Are they believable? Are they persuasive? Are they friendly?
- Do you think they are compatible with your organization? Are they savvy? How do you rate their soft skills (ability to initiate and maintain conversations, be comfortable in social settings, communicate their skills and reason for being at the organization within a short sound bite, and so on)? Are they astute? Do they understand different organizational cultures? What is their experience?
- What do they know about your organization? How do they know that information? What are they curious about? What is their perception of the ease or challenge of the project?
- Do they have the expertise to do the job at your organization? Have they had specific experience with the project? Have they had specific experience with the type, size, and style of your organization?
- Do they have the time to do the job the way you need the job done? Have they been responsive? Are they available when you call? Is it easy to schedule an appointment?
- Are you excited about hiring them? Do you think others will become excited? Will they be easy to sell? Do you really think they will make a difference? Will their energy be infectious?

How Do You Get the Most Return on Investment from a Consultant?

Consultants and speakers are an important investment. How can you make the most of this experience? It is important to consider this question before you contract with the consultant. Know the fee structure of the professional and be clear on what is being asked. Also understand their value on the market and what you would be willing to invest after a positive experience with the professional. Plan on a long-term relationship to create a foundation for future discussions when ideas, questions, and opportunities may arise. Creating a mutually beneficial relationship allows the consultant to value working with you and your organization as an investment in his or her own development. Beyond relationships however, there are steps you can take to ensure that you receive a return on your investment in the services of a consultant or speaker:

- Identify deliverables and particular challenges and concerns
- Identify expectations of communications—how many and how long
- Identify the definition of success and what it takes to achieve it
- Insist on a review of all materials and run through the program before it is presented
- Identify any follow-up and timetable beyond the major event or scope of the project

How Do You Get the Best Performance from a Consultant?

Most consultants and speakers offer a menu of services or presentations. They are usually based on prior performances and popular successes. This may or may not be specifically what you need. You must study the consultant or speaker, their background, expertise, resources, and menu and decide what works best for your organization, regardless of whether it is an offered or stated item on their professional "menu." Ask for what you need, want, and like, the way you want it.

- Brainstorm with them and tell them what would be perfect for your organization
- Ask what is possible
- Ask if they would consider adding elements from other programs
- Ask if they would collaborate
- Ask if they would use internal materials
- Ask for a custom program
- Ask them to interview and meet with some of your organization's stakeholders

Could There Be Mutual Development?

There is the potential for mutual development in establishing a long-term relationship with speakers and consultants. Much of this potential depends on the consultant or speaker and the services represented as well as his or her successes with the organization. Continuity has value because it allows for responsive development in programs. There will be times when a new voice and fresh perspective will be needed. Notwithstanding, programs that are continuous need to adjust to feedback, penetration of targeted groups, change in audience, and other factors. A good speaker or consultant who returns to the same organization is always looking to keep that presentation fresh, responsive to new developments in the organization, and relevant. Long-term relationships with speakers and consultants should continuously challenge their status quo and seek to provide new opportunities for learning and development. This can happen when the diversity professional and consultant or speaker become partners in developing better products and outcomes. Consider the following suggestions to promote mutual development:

- Keep regular communications
- Constantly evaluate
- Continue to read articles and books on relevant topics and discuss them with the consultant or speaker
- Discuss new developments in activities and best practices
- Discuss long-term trajectories of work
- Develop a wish list of future projects
- Ask for suggestions and ideas

Consultants are an investment in your organization's diversity and inclusion initiatives. Programs can vary and cover multiple diversity areas and topics. Thoroughly vetting the consultant and comparing the services he or she provides with the needs of your organization are paramount for a successful relationship and a valuable deliverable for your organization.

What You Should Know

- Know what you want from the consultant and be clear in your instructions. Be prepared to invest time with them to develop a program that is customized to your needs.
- Understand if you can stretch this consultant. Do they have the capacity to go beyond their regular menu of services? Have you seen them adapt or develop new materials specific to a group?
- Plan extra time in all aspects to reduce your anxiety. You are relying on an outsider to make you look good at your job and to meet a specific need. If they are late in delivering anything—their presence, their materials, etc.—you will need to manage it. Give yourself a cushion.
- Continually articulate your goals with the consultant to ensure there is no confusion.
- Work to grow with your consultant as you, the organization, and the needs evolve. A continuing relationship with a consultant that is effective is desirable.
- Be sure to have them sign a confidential agreement at the start of the relationship.
- If multiple consultants present at a program, conference or retreat, make sure that the access of one consultant to another's program is clearly communicated and understood. In other words, notice should be given to a consultant if another consultant or a competitor is attending their session at your event.

CHAPTER 13

RETREATS

Or organizational gatherings that can be really effective

Overview

Many organizations, including large legal organizations, are no strangers to retreats. Many legal organizations have annual partner and senior lawyer retreats, and/or meetings by practice groups or area. Usually, they are designed and developed to foster community, understand and appreciate shared opportunities, challenges, and information, and provide moments to connect, educate, and strategize. Retreats often afford opportunities to connect to become better educated, developed, and informed while also providing forums to address strategies and management of issues.

In the last five years, a growing number of law firms have sponsored retreats focusing on an affinity group or other group under the diversity umbrella. Whether by gender, race, ethnicity, LGBT status, disability, or any other combination of these categories, such retreats can and do provide tremendous value to strengthen organizational and group connections. They provide opportunities for strategic and tactical discussions on important issues and renewed energy with regard to achieving stated goals. Other ancillary benefits include developing a real appreciation of the support and depth of the attorneys who share the diversity goals. In large organizations, it is an opportunity for the participants to get to know each other, which supports the identification and development of future firm leadership. Over time, retreats can be an effective and powerful retention tool.

This section will explore the elements of producing a successful affinity group/inclusion network retreat. Included in this section is a discussion of objectives and goals, agenda, themes, education, structure, guests, and execution and follow-up. The discussion will examine the identified group leaders, who should be invited and why, the role of firm leaders, and whether practice group involvement and structure is important. Awareness of the retreat placement on the organization's diversity continuum is also discussed for program development as well as follow-up.

WHERE TO START

Objectives and goals are important to the success of the retreat. After all, this will be how it is judged. The objectives and goals should be the very measurement of the success of the retreat. The most fundamental question is why should we have a retreat and what would it mean to diversity constituent groups. In essence, what is the point of the retreat? Take a candid assessment of why there is a need for the retreat and understand it from all of the diversity constituents' perspectives. Even if this is not your first retreat, what is the reason, other than repetition and history, for the retreat? (Repeat retreats and continuums of retreats will be discussed later in this section.) Understanding the real needs and wants of the organization will help frame the education, theme, and agenda. It may be good to do some limited formal inquiry, whether by survey or focus group. The following sections will discuss potential reasons to hold a retreat and ways to ensure that you also have input from all aspects of your identified constituents, as well as those you have identified as the participant.

SHOULD WE HAVE A RETREAT?

There are several common scenarios organizations encounter when thinking about reasons to hold a retreat. Below are questions all diversity professionals and organization leaders should be asking in order to determine the value of the retreat and how it will serve diversity needs.

"We have never had a retreat and many key women leaders are very interested in the idea." Consider the answers to the following when planning a retreat:

- What is the retreat in the minds of the women participants? Select a representative group of these women and ask important questions that will assist in understanding their expectations. Have they ever participated in a retreat? What have they heard about retreats, and from whom?
- What are their perspectives and areas of interest? Who are they? What committees do they represent? What practice group, offices, and key clients? Do they have the gravitas to get the decision and budget to have a retreat?
- What is their operational style and what is the best delivery of information for them to support the development of a retreat?

Retreats may also be considered in response to organizational changes. "We have had some recent challenges and some firm leaders and diversity leaders, formal or informal, think that coming together would be helpful and healing." Challenges may include recent departures, changes in leadership, or an incident in the workplace. Important issues to identify and address include:

- Will it be possible to manage this difficult situation and provide an honest, positive, and supportive forum to solicit ideas and strategies for solutions? This should not be a complaint forum.
- Planning this retreat requires sensitivity in the identification of the planning group, the program, and the process by which information is solicited and disseminated.
- It is essential that firm leadership is solidly supportive through attendance and communication with other firm leaders. Without this visible support, all parties involved should clarify their goals and objectives and determine what is realistic without this support.

Retreats may also be held to solidify the organization's diversity efforts. "We want to be serious about our diversity. We are novices but serious learners and this is what we have heard is a best practice. We do not have any affinity groups." Be prepared to understand and appreciate these realities:

- Retreats are hard work. In addition to diversity professionals, you will need a working committee of member volunteers. Members of this group should include leaders who have firm gravitas.
- Do you have firm or company resources that are available for other retreats? Find and use institutional resources, such as meeting planners or project managers, to keep this retreat on par with all others (budget, staff, etc.).
- Solicit as much information as possible about expectations and cast a wide net for the solicitation of ideas, expectations, roadblocks, landmines, successes, possible precedents, opportunities, and so on. The more you know, the better you will manage expectations for the first retreat.
- Identify an informal cabinet to help gauge reality and progress as you navigate the big picture of developing a retreat agenda and structure. This should be a very small group that can provide honest, unfiltered feedback.
- Plan to have fun and make everything about it exciting! Start strong with the positive potential, and the heavy lifting will be easier in this context. Make sure that the first communications to firm leaders, attorneys, and so on include the positive excitement.
- Be prepared for a minimum of nine months of planning. And oftentimes an outside client general counsel may require a longer lead time to accept a speaking engagement. Whether the retreat is at a remote site or within the city, give significant notice for maximum attendance potential.
- Although not necessary, consider a consultant for your first retreat. This kind of professional can facilitate consensus when identifying goals and objectives. A consultant can also assist in connecting the agenda, panels, and programs with the theme and educational outcomes expected.
- This first retreat can be an opportunity to develop affinity groups. This is an important task as a singular goal. It requires additional work that is addressed in Chapter 10. The retreat can provide the first meeting of an affinity group, which is a very powerful and effective beginning.

Retreats may also provide an effective platform to advance leadership goals. "We have been serious about our diversity. We have made significant investments with a professional leader, manager, or director. We have been successful with many development efforts; we have affinity groups, diversity committee(s), and we are deciding if this is a good time (or we have decided it is a good time) to have a retreat. We are not sure who we should include and how often, and if there is there any downside to coming together to discuss our difficult, continual problems?" Consider all of the above with the other sections, but be mindful of the following:

- Understand the budget ramifications. Retreats cost money. The return on the investment is high but there are significant costs. Determine the costs your company or firm budgets per person for retreats. Multiply it by the number of attendees and that is close to your budget. What are the company's or firm's financial strategies for expenditures for the next two years? Is this consistent with those strategies? Is this a big request? Is this the best use of those funds for diversity efforts at this time?
- Why is it important to have a retreat at this time? Will it be responsive to some of the critical issues and challenges identified by the diversity constituents?
- If a retreat is an important part of managing some of the challenges and opportunities for the organization, then it is important to be prepared to study and understand how to present these challenges and opportunities. Regardless of the issue, significant research with reliable data must be available to provide history, context, progression, perspectives, and solutions. This means that the professionals working on the retreat will need to ensure there is significant briefing information that allows everyone involved in strategic solutions to have the same information and the same starting point.
- There is always a potential downside to coming together if the leaders and their communications are not positive and optimistic about the retreat. If a positive and supportive experience is one of the objectives, then every planning aspect should reflect that energy and work against any outliers who may not share the same positive goals.

"We have had previous retreats that were successful. We need to make sure that this next retreat adds additional value to the previous retreats, which will prevent these retreats from becoming a pro forma experience." Successive retreats should become a part of a diversity continuum. Consider:

- What have you learned from previous retreats, both substantively and structurally?
- Are there any consistent themes? Is there a natural progression or expectation of the next step? Were there items that did not make the agenda that were missed at the previous retreats? Did you make a file on "things to consider for the next retreat"?
- What is the overall goal? Retention? Community? Personal and professional development? Firm investment? Assess what the next steps should be as a follow-up to previous seminars, panels, speakers, affinity meetings, practice group sessions, meetings with leaders, and so on.
- Brainstorm on this retreat and retreats in the future. Thinking about a retreat that is two retreats away can give you perspective on long-term goals. These goals can provide a foundation for what to consider for the current agenda as a means to achieve those long-term goals.
- Who has been a leader and who needs leadership development? Use the retreats to highlight attorneys for development. Put them in strategic planning positions with key leaders, provide speaking opportunities, and give them subcommittee ownership for key issues and programs on the agenda.
- Review prior agendas and possible future objectives and goals with diversity constituents and firm leadership. Get feedback from them and ownership of a trajectory, and develop programming with both short-term and long-term goal perspectives.

Who Is Invited and Why?

Internal invitations can be a very important policy decision. They can be based on affinity groups, seniority, or positions in the organization. Here are important considerations:

- If the retreat is gender-based, will it include all attorneys? Does this include temporary, contract, or nonpartnership attorneys? What about attorneys who do not practice law but have professional functions, such as professional development, conflict management, pro bono decision making, or marketing or finance?
- If the retreat is more inclusive than gender, which groups are included? Do you have ethnically centered affinity groups? Traditionally underrepresented groups include African American, Latino/Hispanic, Asian American and South Asian, Middle Eastern (although not an EEOC category for U.S. government reporting), Native American/Alaska Native, and Hawaiian Pacific. Attorneys with these self-identifications may be one of the categories of invitees.
- Gay, lesbian, bisexual, and transgendered attorneys are also an underrepresented group that could be invited, however, their numbers may not be high enough for a retreat exclusive to this group. Some organizations include this group with the above-mentioned groups, sometimes identified as lawyers of color.
- Lawyers with disabilities should also be considered and invited. When developing a retreat with more than one category, be vigilant and aware of all needs, and develop programming that is inclusive both substantively and structurally. (For example, do not schedule LGBT, lawyers with disabilities, and ethnic affinity groups at the same time—some should not have to choose one or the other.)
- Who else is on the outside looking in? Do you have a few international attorneys who may be included with sufficient planning and budgeting time? Are there recent veterans returning to your workplace?

When considering external invitations, defer to the organization's protocols.

- Will clients and outside guests or speakers be invited? If so, put the following concerns on the agenda and discuss them after you understand the firm protocols.
- Will clients and outside guests be allowed to participate in all sessions, or just where they are speaking? Will their presence at some workshops or panels have an impact on honest and open communication? Is there a potential that some workshops or panels may be off-limits to guests?
- Be clear about expenses with clients and guests. Make sure any gratuitous gestures such as travel costs, thank you gifts, charitable donations, etc.,are consistent with the client's ethical protocols.
- Will outside consultants be allowed to attend the other consultants' workshops? Make sure that each consultant knows who is in the audience and if any potential competitors could be present. Also, all consultants should sign confidentiality agreements.
- The attorney acting as the client lead should follow protocols when inviting outside guests. Be sure to communicate to guests on any panel the names, companies, and titles of others who are invited to be on their panel. Make sure all communication is through the client lead or outside counsel lead unless different protocols are established.

Other external invitations that must be considered include the personal guests of your attendees:

- Will spouses be allowed?
- Will children be allowed?
- Are attorneys expected to attend all functions involving food without guests?
- Will there be any time or activities that can be inclusive of personal guests?

SOLICITING INPUT

Now it is important to identify what your attendees want from a retreat. While this information does not need to be determinative, it is crucial data for developing structure and content. There are some easy ways to gather this information. Your affinity group leadership can be invaluable in gathering information. If your firm or department utilizes surveys consider using this system to solicit input. If there are no existing meetings with available time, then try a brown bag lunch with free dessert and drinks or an afternoon beverage break to ask folks what they would like in a retreat. The following questions can be used as a foundation for a survey or a discussion:

- What subjects should be covered at our retreat?
- What skills would you like to develop at the retreat?
- What leaders would you like to hear from or meet at the retreat?
- What was the best part of any retreat you have ever attended?
- Is social time important for the retreat? Should it be structured?
- Do you think it is important to meet by practice group? By affinity? By office?
- Do you think clients should be invited to speak at or participate in the retreat?
- Are there firm policies/procedures/information that need more clarification?
- Are there firm functions that should have time at the retreat (recruitment, professional development, pro bono)?

Quick surveys or a month designated for a "retreat idea solicitation meeting" in each office can provide a laundry list of ideas that can be sorted into manageable categories that could become the subjects of particular panels. Sorting the information into categories is critical in managing and meeting expectations. Categories that naturally evolve are professional development, business development, firm functions and information, and leadership, personal empowerment, and development. Keeping it organized by categories also allows future planning in the follow-up stage. The following table provides examples of ideas that could be identified and categories for sorting:

Professional Development	Business Development	Firm Functions
Time management/ethics	Cross-selling within firm	Partner compensation process
Organizational savviness	Developing clients	Associate evaluation process
Networking	Client CLEs	Firm membership committee

Equally important are the leadership's ideas and perspectives on the retreat. While the person who has the final decision on the program may vary, it will be important to formally or informally solicit ideas and input from your diversity leaders and diversity partners, as well as those who support your activities on a regular basis. This would include committee leaders, impact committee leaders, and the leaders of recruitment, human resources, professional development, library services, and associate evaluations.

RETREAT LEADERSHIP STRUCTURE

Once you have as much input as possible, structure is critical. Who will the decision makers be? How large and manageable will that group be? Is there a way to structure maximum input with efficient decision making that allows the retreat workers to be as nimble as possible when planning? This can be institution specific; however, there are a few models that can provide fundamental templates a firm or department can tailor to its specific needs.

Large Input Solicitation Committee/Smaller Advisory Group/Small Pragmatic Decision Makers

A large input solicitation committee can be the firm-wide diversity committee or a task force with representatives in each office who can solicit information from each of the targeted perspectives identified, for example, by office, practice group, or affinity group. You can solicit this group directly through the diversity committee or use the task force to gather information from each constituent area. The smaller advisory group, specific to the retreat, should manage the information that is collected from the larger group, including categorizing the information, researching subject areas, and identifying speakers and panelists. This group can mold the substance as well as the structure, and funnel the information to the small, pragmatic decision makers. The pragmatic decision makers could be the affinity group chairs, the diversity committee chair, and the subcommittee leaders. The decision-making group should be very small and is charged with making pragmatic decisions based on previous input and the goals and objectives. The group should make decisions on a weekly basis and then ultimately make daily decisions as the retreat approaches.

Large Input Solicitation Committee/Large Advisory Group/ Smaller Pragmatic Decision Maker or Diversity Professional

This large input committee is the same as the one just discussed, however, there is also a diversity committee or another large committee that will remain involved in the process through agenda development and implementation. Managing a large group while developing a consensus and program can be difficult. If a consultant has not been engaged, consider developing a committee structure arranged by retreat function and keep the smaller groups focused with specific tasks and timetables. You will still need to have a smaller pragmatic decision-making group, but you will also have to manage the democratic process of involving the larger group while breaking down tasks, responsibilities, and roles. Once your retreat work has evolved into real day-to-day decisions, you must employ practices that allow your larger group awareness of the decisions but do not allow them to make the process cumbersome. The smaller pragmatic decision-making group can be one of the subgroups that is identified by the larger advisory group or the diversity professional.

Large Advisory Group/Key Leaders and Diversity Professional

This can be very similar to the first model, with the leader of a small affinity group in charge. A large advisory group that can provide input and reactions is also invaluable to this model. Working with key leaders and the diversity professional will provide a nimble approach to making real-time decisions, as the process of planning requires on-the-spot decisions and the development of personal relationships. This can be a very efficient process, however, it is important to ensure that you are getting enough input from the targeted smaller constituent groups, for example, various offices, practice groups, and affinity groups.

Key Firm Leaders/Input and Solicitation Collective or Professional

This can be the most nimble of all groups, but can also be the most disconnected. You should still work hard to solicit input based on the previously discussed models. Also, focus on whose definition of success will be considered and at what levels. Are the definitions of success by the leaders and those who attend the retreat the same? If different, how can the retreat accommodate both? Consider these kinds of issues with a small planning group while you are planning. Do not plan in a high-end silo.

ASSESSMENT OF NEEDS

Once you have amassed as much input as you can from individual lawyers, office groups, practice groups, affinity groups, firm leaders, diversity department partners, and anybody else you can solicit, you must categorize the information to understand what it is your participants want. Step back and try to understand their needs, beyond *your* vision of their needs.

- Are the attendees stating a need for personal development (time management, stress management, leadership)?
- Are they identifying a void for professional development (a need to meet in practice groups to understand their development and potential)? Do they want to understand how to be a better lawyer at the firm?
- Is there a need for a better understanding of firm functions? How compensation really works? How matters are opened and how credit is shared? What is really important in the associate evaluation

process? What are the firm resources and how does one really get on a committee?
- Is there a strong need for time to get together without an agenda? Are people really asking for networking time? Time to get to know each other and their practice?
- What are the needs and can all of these needs be met in one retreat?
- If not, what are the overarching concerns identified in the initial survey process regarding why there is a need for a retreat? How do you address those concerns based on the input received and the needs you have identified from the earlier process of soliciting input?

Use your leadership groups and structure to help make the difficult decisions regarding what can and cannot be managed in this retreat. Remember, if you strategize in the context of the next two retreats, you can plan to include these issues for next time. Make lists in categories and have a few discussions with your smaller pragmatic group to prioritize the subjects with rankings. This will allow easier planning when a list of important subjects for panels and seminars is required.

Education

Now that there is a list of subjects with priority ranking, go back to your goals and objectives. Why is this being done? What needs to happen for this retreat to be considered a success? How will you educate *everyone* who comes to the retreat? There should be educational goals for each of your constituents who will be attending the retreat.

- What do the associates and junior lawyers need to learn? What has been identified as topics these groups need to appreciate and understand? How can associates educate partners, practice group leaders, and firm leaders on issues that affect them?
- What do senior lawyers and partners need to learn? How can they communicate their needs for successful development to the practice

group and firm leaders? How can they educate the associates and other attendees with their experience and wisdom?
- What will the firm leaders learn? What do they need to know and understand to successfully develop and retain their attorneys? How can this retreat help them understand the systemic challenges to the success of their attorneys? Their organization?
- What can the department leaders learn? What can representatives from recruiting, pro bono, professional development, and marketing learn from this retreat? Will there be opportunities to explore a more effective and efficient way of working together?

After this exploration and understanding with your smaller pragmatic group, begin to identify possible panels or seminars. List topics and potential speakers. Review the subject matter and speakers and determine if there are any opportunities to obtain CLE credit for any of the workshops. Work with firm resources to determine what is required for each jurisdiction and be sure to communicate if a CLE application is pending.

Agenda

The agenda is the logical extension of the panels and speakers. Once you have identified the substance of the panels and listed the priorities, you can begin to create a structure. Consider:

- How many days will the retreat last?
- Can scheduled meal-time functions serve as potential speaking or panel opportunities?
- Can a meal-related program provide an opportunity for unstructured time for planned or unplanned activities needed for informal networking?
- Consider the opening and closing, which typically have the fewest attendees. How can you make sure the opening is strong enough to attract as many people as possible, and that the closing is at a time that does not conflict with most departures?
- Will there be many plenary sessions for everyone or will there be seminars tailored to specific interests or needs?

- Will there be seminars based on tenure tracking? Will junior, mid-level, and senior lawyers and associates have programming specific to them? What about of counsel and partners?
- How will the scheduling allow maximum participation and include as many attendees as possible?
- Will there be time for affinity group meetings? Will there be time to meet by business or practice group? What about by office?
- Should you consider a town hall or open mic session to suggest subjects?
- Will you have assigned seating at food functions? Should you consider progressive seating, with firm leaders rotating tables?
- Do you need ice breakers at receptions?
- Should you structure time with leaders—perhaps a plenary session?
- Have you considered any opportunities the hospitality suite can provide for informal networking and fellowship?

Theme

The theme is the essence of the retreat in a sound bite. It should be established, stated, and repeated often. Remember, the theme is the driving force. It is what people will think of when reflecting upon the success of the retreat. Open with the theme, mention it at every food function, and close with the theme; discuss how the retreat, seminars, and planned and unplanned activities contribute to the theme of the retreat. It will be the mantra through which the attendees will understand why they are there and what their individual goals and objectives should be. Make sure that the theme is in every communication and on every agenda. It is an important part of creating an expectation, but also will inform the group regarding how to develop their personal objectives for the retreat.

Execution

The execution of the retreat is similar to planning a large meeting. In addition to working with a meeting planner who will assist in the identification of a hotel or meeting space, catering, and audio/visual and technical needs, take a project manager approach with realistic and strict timetables. Like hosting a good party, your hosts for the retreat should be relaxed and gracious to set the tone for an exciting and positive retreat. Follow these tips for a successful retreat:

- Consider using a consultant.
- Identify outside speakers 9 to 12 months from the date of the retreat.
- Plan to have the program finalized, with speakers, two months before the retreat.
- Be sure to send a save the date nine months in advance.
- Continue to send reminders and updates.
- Use the firm or company leaders to send communications to practice group leaders, office managing partners, and others announcing the retreat and its importance.
- Get on the firm or company leader's calendar six to nine months in advance to ensure they can attend.
- Keep goals and objectives on flip chart paper in office.
- Plan each day on flip chart paper.
- Put a timetable on the flip chart and keep it in front of the team and committees; constantly evaluate whether the retreat is on schedule.

FOLLOW-UP

The need to follow up is crucial. One way to appreciate what follow-up is needed is to evaluate each session. As you may know, if there is CLE credit pending, immediate evaluations are necessary. Immediate paper evaluations can be cumbersome, but may be better than waiting to survey attendees electronically. You will get more paper evaluations in real time than responses to a post-retreat online survey.

You may also want to explore voluntary scribes for each session. These are attorneys who have been asked to take notes for the sessions they attend. You can provide packets with lined paper or they can take notes on computers and electronically submit them. It is critical to get these notes transcribed and put into a final report about the retreat. Any ideas or suggestions you need to follow up on should be flagged and listed separately on a follow-up sheet. If practice group sessions met, and the sessions were not confidential, send the notes to the practice group leader. Write a final retreat report on all aspects of the retreat, including attendance, budget, goals, theme, agenda, program, scribe notes, evaluations, and follow-up.

Tips for Retreats

- Make a picture book of attendees with abbreviated biographies for all attorneys in designated groups for the retreat.
- Use a buddy system that pairs new attorneys with attorneys who have had a longer tenure with the organization.
- Consider having some fun activities during a reception or at the hospitality suite—they can break down barriers and make connections among different groups of attorneys.

Retreats are hard work. They take a lot of time and are a great investment in retention. Usually, attorneys are excited about attending retreats and bring positive energy and enthusiasm to the event. The return can be amazing. Attorneys leave feeling good about the organization, excited about their future with the organization, and enthusiastic about their law practice and career future. Very few other organizational programs or initiatives can accomplish such high level of intangible benefits within a few days. Retreats are the field of dreams—they show that the sum is greater than the parts and that there are people at the organization who want to invest in the success of the participants. However, retreats are only as effective as the leadership investment and the personal follow-up. Plan carefully.

What You Should Know

- As soon as you establish a date, send a save-the-date to constituents and leaders.
- Be clear that this will be a positive gathering that will add value to all attending. Then determine how.
- Solicit input from everyone. After save-the-date, send out a simple survey that asks about expectations and needs. Use that as your guide.
- Define success early and communicate it early and often. "This is a gathering to connect and get to know each other." "This is designed to educate about organizational systems and structure." "This is to facilitate professional development, business development, and connections across the organization."
- Enlist the support and participation of leaders and allies within the organization.
- Survey and evaluate as soon as possible. Provide a report.

CHAPTER 14

METRICS: THE MEASURE OF SUCCESS

Or what matters is measured and what is measured matters

Overview

A metric system is a key component of a diversity initiative. A few questions to ask include: What is the importance of measuring the composition, succession, distribution, projections, and realities of your organization? Why would or should you collect, analyze, distribute, and review data? Data will give you historical and present-day snapshots of your organization. It is an important tool in making projections and plays a critical role in the diversity development of an organization.

To understand data, you must first understand your organization's systems, structure, titles, and processes, which will differ from organization to organization. You must have a working knowledge of your organization's hiring, evaluation, compensation, promotion, and leadership selection systems. Further, you must understand the published and political hierarchies. You must know all the titles and the trajectories of each and should appreciate the finance, human resources, and data collection processes. Finally, you must know the questions to ask to obtain the information you need to make accurate measurements and assessments.

Data is most important if it is studied and used to educate organizational leaders on the diversity realities of the organization. In this section, we will examine the mechanics of data, what to collect, how, and why, the questions to ask, the value of the data, the publication and use of the data, and examples of how data can play a critical role in diversity development.

The Mechanics of Data

The mechanics of data examines how, what, and why data is gathered. The following are some questions to consider regarding the mechanics of your data:

- What data do you need most? What information is on the top ten request lists?
- How many lawyers are in your organization?
- What is the gender composition?
- What ethnicities are represented?
- How large is your LGBT community?
- Do you track lawyers with disabilities? If so, what is the data?
- What geographic areas are lawyers located?
- What practices do they represent?
- What levels of seniority do they have?
- Who are the leaders in the firm?
- Who are the members of the important committees and decision-making committees?
- Who are we hiring?
- Who is leaving?
- Who is staying? Who is promoted?
- Who gets bonuses? Who doesn't?
- Who is reaching the annual billable hours requirement, if any? Who isn't?
- Who receives the highest performance reviews? Who receives the lowest?
- Who participates in pitches and is identified in RFPs?

How do you collect this data? In addition to working with your strategic partners in finance and human resources, you must understand how your organization collects data generally and where and why the data is compiled and stored. It is important to establish a fundamental knowledge of a shared language with your data partners. You need to understand if a particular data pool is head count, full time equivalents (FTEs), or timekeepers. You must be aware of the differences and the impact analysis. For example, if you have a significant number of women who are not FTEs, that data pool will not include them, but they will be included in the head count data pool. Timekeepers may include paralegals or other employees who are not lawyers. Finance and human resources teams may operate with different data pools. Is the financial information compatible with human resources information? Is there one system of data that keeps performance, hours and demographic data such as gender, LGBT and ethnicity? How often is such information updated in the system? What data pools and systems does the marketing department use, if any, to track RFPs and pitches?

It is important to regularly collect, review, and publish data both internally and externally. Many external publications, bar associations, and/or clients or reporting authorities request data on a regular basis. How should data be managed internally? How often should you review data and what data should be reviewed on a regular basis? Who reviews it?

Monthly Data Recommendations

The following data should be collected and reviewed monthly:

- Overall numbers: total population, with all categories (to include gender, ethnicity, LGBT, disability, and veteran status)
- Overall numbers by location with the same categories
- Overall numbers by practice area or department with the same categories
- Further breakdown of ethnic categories (not included in the EEOC categories) such as South Asian and Middle Eastern
- Comprehensive list of all lawyers in all categories, including practice area, location, and tenure with organization
- Comprehensive list of all hires and all departures
- Billable hours pace or other performance-based assessment of junior to senior lawyers and associates

Quarterly Data Recommendations

The following data should be collected and reviewed quarterly:

- Pitch and RFP data reports for all categories (to include gender, ethnicity, LGBT, and disability status)
- Billable hours or performance on top clients and top matters by lawyer demographics
- Hires
- Departures

Annual Data Recommendations

The following data should be collected and reviewed annually:

- Leadership composition by demographics
- Identify demographics of practice group leaders, department leaders, office leaders, and executive and management committees
- Committee composition by demographics
- The composition of impact/decision-making committees
- Evaluations or quantitative assessments of trajectories (on track for partnership, directorships, bonuses, performance bonuses)
- Executive/partner compensation
- Salary review and assessment of any disparities
- Attrition rates for the practice and by department, location, demographics (gender, ethnicity, LGBT, and disability), and tenures
- Retention rates for the practice and by department, location, demographics, and tenures
- Exit interview data, if available

Why do you need this data? It will provide you with the tools to assess status and progress, to understand challenges and opportunities, and to evaluate and develop solutions. Studying this data will provide the answers to critical questions that are necessary and inevitable when evaluating, developing, or assessing diversity efforts in any organization.

Additional Questions to Consider

- What percentage of executives or partners are women? What percentage of junior lawyers or associates are women? What percentage of leaders in general are women? Is the organization's overall percentage of women the same as the percentage of women in leadership, executive/partner ranks, or at the higher compensation levels?
- Ask the same questions regarding ethnicity. What is the data for each specific ethnicity?
- What are those percentages for disabled and LGBT employees?
- Is the organization led and managed by the same demographic percentages represented in the overall population?
- Who is working for the top clients and on high-profile matters? What are the demographics of the client leads and project leads for those high-profile matters? Who are the top billers for such clients and who puts in top hours for highly visible key matters?
- Who is being identified for client contact with pitches?
- Who is being identified in RFPs?
- Does the organization track the status of RFPs and audit whether those identified in the RFP are actually assigned the work on the matter when the business is obtained or assigned?
- Who is being identified for key teams? How is that work distributed and monitored?
- What is the demographic composition of the higher compensation levels?
- Who is performing on pace? Who is not? What are their practice areas? Where are they located?
- Is there any correlation between the demographics of departures and practice areas and/or locations?
- Is there any correlation between the demographics of promotions and practice areas and/or locations?
- Are there any concerns raised by the evaluation processes?
- Are there any concerns regarding retention at particular tenure points? Are lawyers departing at a particular tenure period?

- Are there representational issues in any practice area, department or location? Perhaps there are no women in executive roles or with partner status. Perhaps there are practice areas, departments, or location with a particular ethnicity that is not represented or a "lonely only."
- What are departing lawyers citing as reasons for leaving? Is there any data suggesting that a disproportionate amount of departures reside in a particular practice area, department, or location?

The Value of Data

The value of comprehensive data is significant. It is most valuable to the organization and to advancing diversity and inclusion goals when the diversity practitioner studies the data and makes an analysis. After the questions have been asked and the data collected, the study and analysis must begin. The diversity professional must review historical data and regularly review new data. If data is collected regularly, a comparative analysis should be part of the periodic process. Study and review the month-to-month data to discern if any trends are developing. Quarterly data should be reviewed on a rolling year-to-year basis, comparing quarters to quarters (e.g., compare Q1 2012 to Q1 2011). Annual data should be assessed each year and then in three-, four-, and five-year increments. The data must be studied and reviewed and then put in the context of the organization's diversity efforts. The data also should be evaluated for trends, peaks, valleys, and a steady pace, up or down. It should be viewed as a tool for education; it is the foundation for new policies and programs and it provides direction for future diversity efforts.

The data establishes a baseline for assessment. This assessment will tell the story of successes and challenges. It has often been said that "what gets measured, gets done." The data will reveal where work is needed and where systems have been effective and ineffective. It will show the status of the organization's overall diversity representation, what can be expected, and if there is more work to be done in certain areas, such as recruitment efforts. The data will tell you where to concentrate certain efforts and will illuminate if certain groups are not being included and where. It will identify patterns and trends with respect to who is leaving and from which departments or locations. This will help you to discern if your data represents a recruitment issue or a retention issue. In other words, are you bringing the attorneys in, but not keeping them, or are the attorneys staying, but you are not recruiting with high levels of diversity?

The evaluation process data will help you understand the performances of your lawyers by demographic. It will show who is performing well, who is receiving merit bonuses, if applicable, and who is receiving production bonuses, from the perspective of gender, race, LGBT status, and other diversity areas. The data will also identify those who are underperforming and their practice areas and offices. A careful study will show whether there are any trends with performance that correlate with tenure, office, practice areas, demographics, and any combination thereof.

An analysis of the data pipeline will show leadership and promotion projections. It will reveal whether there are people from underrepresented groups who are in a position to ascend to leadership or key committees. Further, it will assist you in identifying opportunities for placement on key committees and in leadership development programs. The data will establish trends and will show who has served on committees and in leadership roles, and who is available. If there is no apparent pool, then the data will reveal exactly where to start building the pipeline and how long it will take through organic growth, without lateral hire intervention. The data also will reveal deficiencies in particular tenure statuses, whether midlevel, senior, or partner/executive, and the impact of those deficiencies on diversity efforts. The data will help you to examine the nature and timing of the pipeline, which can be critical in shaping future decisions.

Another key area in which the data is critical is with respect to RFPs, client pitches, and access to key clients and matters. The data will identify patterns and trends with respect to who has had opportunities to work on RFPs, pitches, and key client or high-profile matters. The data will provide information on the number of RFPs or pitches and who has been identified in these efforts. It will also tell you about demographic representation among the lawyers identified in the RFP and whether there is a pattern of repeat names, that is, whether the same people are typically identified for RFPs. A system of data collection will also tell you if those identified in the RFP actually received the work when the firm or department was successful, and who is most active in leading RFPs by attorney, practice group, department, and office. This is important information when raising awareness and fashioning remedies to the challenges identified through the study of such data.

Compensation data is often extremely sensitive both in terms of confidentiality and from a risk management perspective. Notwithstanding, this data can be aggregated discretely and is critical in identifying the presence of disparities and determining whether there may be systemic issues in promotion, access to key client and high-profile opportunities, or other systems that can affect compensation. (For example, in a law firm, how a client matter is opened; how credit is distributed among partners/lawyers, etc.) Further, the study of compensation can be at the junior/associate or the executive/partner level. Discoveries regarding compensation require high-level examination, as these are highly confidential and important areas.

Issues regarding practice areas and office locations can also be examined. Such an examination may include the overall compensation, the leadership, the clients, the demographics of the different levels of tenure, the pipeline, the nature of the evaluations, and the levels of compensation. It will be a story that has both obvious and surprise chapters that will be important to understand and appreciate when implementing programs in the diversity efforts. The study and analysis of this data is a task best done with the leaders of the relevant areas. This will yield mutual appreciation as well as a leader's perspective with a historical context. It will also help create an understanding if there is a need for careful monitoring or intervention—such as a "lonely only" or a potential lateral who would address a particular deficiency (e.g., if there are no female partners, but there is a strong lateral partner candidate who is female). The data will also tell you who is leaving and the groups and offices where there is greater or lesser attorney retention. This could be important information when responding to exit interview information. You can learn why people leave, but you also need to understand why people stay.

The Publication and Use of Data

Let's start with who looks at the data and why. Should all data be made available to anyone internally? How should the dissemination of data be managed? Why is this important? The publication and distribution of data internally must be strategic and done in a manner that ensures there is always integrity with public data. How should the dissemination of data be managed? One person should be the final repository of all data and provide the final draft of the data for approval by the diversity professional. Any and all requests for data, whether a casual request by a practice area leader or a response to a client survey, must go through one central person. This ensures that dissemination of the data is done within the context of all requests; this person knows the difference between requests and the nature of the data pool involved in the response. Using one central person will ensure there is a consistent "apples to apples" comparative analysis or that explanations are provided when different pools of data are used and appear to be inconsistent. For example, the number of lawyers may appear different when using FTE instead of head count, or if the data is limited to U.S. offices rather than being global. Having one person who serves as the focal point for distributing data supports the integrity of the system, diminishes the opportunity for disparity, and increases the ability to quickly resolve misunderstandings.

Who looks at the data and why? There are public sources of information about law firms and, in certain instances, law departments, and certain data is easily retrievable online. There can and should be quick and easy access to this information, for example through the National Association for Law Placement (NALP), American Lawyer Media, Vault, and so on. Information that is not public should be distributed judiciously and strategically. Data should be shared with the executive leadership of the firm. Quarterly reports to the firm or department management can be helpful in the diversity educational process and to practice area and office or department leaders. Further, data should be shared with the leadership of key committees for understanding, awareness, and discussion. By collectively studying the data with these key individuals and groups, the diversity professional can develop better relationships and build support for diversity initiatives within the firm.

Should all data be made available to anyone internally? Is it prudent to provide all the data that is available to the diversity professional to the diversity committee, department, or firm? If the data needs an explanation, then it is probably best to share when it is specifically requested; however, most data needs an explanation. Discussion is always needed when questions arise, for example, as already discussed, regarding the distinction between head count and FTE. Sharing the data that is already public means that everyone has the same data and there is a shared knowledge of the intricacies of such data. Sharing other data that is not public and may be unsolicited can lead to confusion and additional discussion to clarify or explain that data.

Why is it important to always have confidence in the integrity of your data? The diversity professional should have the last look at the data before it is published. This is to ensure that the data is responsive, self-explanatory, and consistent with and/or distinguishable from any other data that is public. Regardless of whether you like the numbers or not, they must be above reproach and the organization must be able to rely on the integrity of its diversity data.

How Data Can Play a Critical Role

Data is a critical tool in your diversity work. It can be the foundation of relationships with firm or department leaders, the impetus for a change in policy or strategic direction, or the story that provides epiphanies on a systemic bottleneck or ineffectiveness. Data is an important element in developing the strategic plan and picture. It will provide the measurement by which you can evaluate programs and processes—a key factor in determining success. Data can also be distracting, confusing, and alienating. It is a powerful tool that should be used with strong analysis and a sensitive perspective. The diversity professional must be careful to use data effectively and without indictment, even if the data is not flattering or provides challenges to a particular area of the organization. An astute diversity professional can create important educational campaigns based on the needs identified in the data. For example, data can raise awareness and strengthen discussions regarding a lack of gender or ethnic diversity in a particular office or location. Data helps to distinguish between a perceived deficit or concern and a deficit or concern that is statistically determined.

What You Should Know

- Always, always ensure that your data has integrity. Check and double check. Errors are unacceptable.
- Try to keep an open mind about what you may learn. Expect to be surprised. If you think you know what the data will tell you, then your bias is already set.
- Run your numbers before you are expected to measure them. If it is annual data, check the trends quarterly. If it is quarterly data, check the monthly information. Do not be caught off guard because you were not looking for trends.
- Ask a lot of different questions about the data to take a comprehensive look at it. Analyze it from others's perspectives. Defend the data. Attack the data. Look at the data from many angles. What does it tell you? What does it tell HR? Recruiting? Etc.
- Ask if you are tracking enough data or too much? Can you explain and rationalize all the data reports your department generates? If not, then do so.
- If the data is not helpful or educational, you must question why it is collected.

CHAPTER 15

GOING GLOBAL

Or it's a small world after all

Overview

Advancing diversity and inclusion in the workplace is not a U.S. phenomenon—it is a global reality. The business case for creating, advancing, and promoting a diverse and inclusive workplace is a global one. Talent management, firm branding, product excellence, broad client access and competition for creativity and innovation are a few of the desired business goals driving the need for diversity and inclusion in today's global business. In the legal sector, many law firms and corporate legal departments continue to advance the ideals of diversity across the globe by actively supporting initiatives to promote a diverse and inclusive business. This is also true of many government agencies.

The concept of diversity will vary and have a different focus based on geography and jurisdiction. The term 'diversity' itself has many connotations. A one-size-fits-all diversity initiative will not address the individual needs of each region or promote inclusion in the organization. The diversity professional must develop a global strategy that is aligned with the overall business objectives of the organization, but must also recognize and make room for the individual diversity needs of each office and location of the organization. The plan will lack veracity if it fails to recognize and include individual needs and goals. As a best practice and matter of good policy, the overall diversity and inclusion mission should be consistent throughout the organization; however, the individual objectives, tactical strategy, and planning needed to accomplish the stated goals must be customized and relevant to each region of business. Again, while the diversity focus will certainly vary in each jurisdiction, the issue of gender diversity and equality is a global concern and worth exploring as a starting point.

HOW TO GET STARTED

A good place to start is by doing some homework. This includes performing an assessment of the region and office in each jurisdiction relevant to the organization and answering the following questions:

- How is diversity perceived?
- Are there any legal considerations?
- Are there data privacy restrictions limiting group identification and the collection of data?
- Is the word "diversity" a part of the nomenclature? Should it be used to describe the initiative?
- What are the cultural considerations?
- What terms are used to describe diversity and inclusion concepts?
- Who are the clients in the region serving as diversity champions?
- What concerns are being raised?
- Are diversity concerns relevant to other industries in the jurisdiction?
- How is diversity being approached and discussed by businesses in the region?
- How is diversity being addressed in the legal community (bar associations, law societies, community organizations) of the region, office, company?
- Is history relevant and how?

Having this background information is a simple and a relatively commonsense approach; however, diversity can often be painted with a broad brush, failing to capture the individual thoughts of the region. There is no substitute for being on the ground in each jurisdiction to obtain a first-hand account of how the organization's diversity and inclusion initiative is being perceived; however, if this is not possible there is much that can be done without being in-person through research and organizational outreach. For example, contacting the local bar association or law society will offer great insight, as well as establishing small local focus groups and discussions.

Listen

Obtaining the perspectives and needs of the people in the region where you are developing the plan is critical to understanding their perspectives and to extending ownership of the initiative. It is important to recognize that issues of culture play a significant role and will impact perception, planning, development, and strategy.

- What are the concerns of those in the office?
- How do members of the office perceive the organization's current diversity and inclusion efforts?
- Do they feel such efforts are applicable to them?
- In what ways do they think the office could be more diverse and inclusive?
- In what ways would they like to participate?

Find a Champion

Start with a plan to find a champion! Who can it be? The diversity champion is a member of the office who can assist with outreach to other members of the office, and in many cases externally as well. The champion can be anyone who wants to advance diversity goals in the office; however, persons who are senior and have influence over other members of the office are often the most effective champions, as law firms and legal departments are often top-down organizations following the lead of the people in the most senior positions. The diversity professional should assist members of the office with plan development, as they are in the best position to determine what may be impactful and helpful in their region.

Develop a List of Objectives and Goals

Identify and focus on regional initiatives that can be implemented—what's trending in the area? How can you use these trends to advance the diversity and inclusion platform? Identify resources, both in terms of human capital and budget. Be prepared to communicate how your diversity initiative can benefit the organization (e.g., if the firm works with any clients who publically promote diversity and inclusion) or the consumers or shareholders who may have concerns or interests. Prepare and prioritize a list of goals. Include how you will evaluate the success of each initiative.

Execute the Plan

Develop a roll-out plan and establish support from internal departments. Internal initiatives should be executed in coordination with members of the office's human resources team, recruiting professionals, development professionals, and marketing and communications professionals. For many offices, one person may serve several functions, but it is important to have the buy-in and resources of those supporting the diversity efforts of the office.

Identify Local Experts

If education awareness is part of the plan, identify local experts and consultants whenever possible. Utilizing consultants and experts from areas outside of the region with whom the diversity professional has worked in the past may be an easy fix from a planning perspective, but often lacks authenticity and relevance to members in that particular region. *Local expertise is always helpful and usually more impactful.* Local experts are also aware of and experienced in diversity and inclusion concerns and challenges of their region and how they are being addressed generally and in the legal and business communities.

COMMUNICATION AND CONTINUITY

Consistent and ongoing communication with members of the office is always a must. Communicating at regular and frequent intervals is critical in helping to establish the diversity professional's presence and support in advancing the diversity and inclusion strategy designed and developed. Working with the office champion will assist in keeping the diversity dialogue present and fresh. In addition, members of the office's administrative support team can help identify local events in the legal and business communities, updating web pages, calendars, and so on to keep office members informed of opportunities. Being on the ground in person is always great, but for many reasons, it may not always be possible. Whenever possible, identify others in your company who may be visiting offices that you cannot visit and ask them to serve as your ambassador.

Remember to include all offices outside of the United States in the U.S. events when possible, for example, including a video or call-in option to participate in programs, hear speakers, and so on. Time zone differences may be less than ideal, however, it is better to offer the option than to summarily exclude other offices. Many organizations often have regional meetings and retreats, which can be the perfect time to include a diversity and inclusion discussion, presentation, or program. It is helpful to make sure the program or discussion is in line with the theme of the meeting or event, serving as a value-add to the entire program.

What You Should Know

- This is country-specific. Know your country. Know the history. Know your office. Know your people.
- Be graceful and gracious. Mistakes are the landmines on the beach. Keep a spirit of inclusion, respectful collaboration, and curiosity and honest faux pas will be forgiven.
- Find your resources. Stay in communication and consult on a consistent basis.
- Continue to educate yourself constantly.

CHAPTER 16

SUPPLIER DIVERSITY

Or diversity helping diversity

Overview

A supplier diversity program is an integral part of a comprehensive diversity and inclusion initiative. In general, it is a business procurement program for goods and services utilizing businesses and enterprises that are at least 51 percent owned, operated, or controlled by underrepresented members of the business community, such as ethnic minorities, women, LGBT persons, veterans and persons with disabilities. Supplier diversity programs incorporate the diversity and inclusion goals into its business procurement process. As a business matter, such initiatives can have a positive impact through increased competition for goods and services, and the opportunity for improved quality, service and pricing.

Following are key steps to establishing a supplier diversity program:

1. *Do your homework:* Research supplier diversity programs, attend conferences on the topic, speak with supplier diversity professionals and gain a clear and comprehensive understanding of the procurement process and how a supplier diversity program will impact the organization's current procurement policies and practices. Developing a supplier diversity program is hard work and requires procurement expertise.
2. *Establish a partnership with your organization's procurement department:* Discuss and align your organization's supplier diversity goals with existing procurement practices. You will need the assistance of the procurement professionals to implement the programs needed to

advance your supplier diversity goals. The procurement team should be a joint partner and champion of this initiative

3. *Develop business objectives:* Define the program to include what it is, why it is important, and how it will impact the organization and contribute to the success of its diversity and inclusion efforts. It is critical to clearly state the business and diversity objectives and goals for the initiative.
4. *Get buy-in and support from senior management:* It is important to have the public support of your organization's senior leadership when implementing this program. This is extremely helpful as the plan is rolled out and participation and support from within the organization is encouraged. The procurement process is often not limited to the members of the procurement department, but may be a function of many throughout the organization
5. *Develop diversity spend goals:* Develop and implement a system to track the supplier diversity spend. Spend will include direct spend, referred to as Tier 1, as well as indirect spend, referred to as Tier 2 spend. Tier 1 spend is procurement directly between the organization and its vendor. Tier 2 spend is attributed to the organization indirectly through the supplier and diversity spend with its vendors. The type of spend that will be included is important when establishing spend goals and priorities. Keeping track of the spend data is an important metric for evaluating the program's success. It is important to also partner with members of your technology department as special programs may be needed to accommodate this new initiative.
6. *Identify areas of procurement:* Consider what goods and services will be included in the program. Law firms and corporations have broad purchasing needs, and thus the goods and services that can be included in the supplier program are extensive. Professional services should also be considered and may include local counsel opportunities, document review needs, accounting services, and so on. When initiating the program, areas of procurement may be limited initially, with planned expansion of goods and services as the program develops.
7. *Identify who will be eligible to participate:* Equally as important is determining the diverse type of businesses that will participate. Will you limit to minority and women-owned businesses or broaden to

include LGBT, veterans, persons with disabilities, small businesses, and others? Clearly, eligibility to participate is critical.

8. *Develop a plan to launch and manage the program:* Develop a detailed plan to implement the program, including initiating partnerships with certifying organizations and developing a supplier database, procurement procedures, and procedures to track procurements. A third party organization may also be utilized to assist with the procurement process and linking the suppliers with the organization and initiating software to develop and track the program. This can be a complex task and should be done in partnership with your organization's procurement and technology professionals.
9. *Market and advertise the program:* Work with the marketing and communications departments to develop a program to advertise the supplier diversity program to potential suppliers outside of the organization, as well as an internal marketing campaign to inform and share the program with members of the organization. This also will include working with your organization's webmaster, as well as your marketing team.
10. *Understand how to determine whether a company is diverse:* They are organizations that certify suppliers as diverse—women or minority owned.

Certifying Organizations to Consider When Developing Strategic Partnerships

- National Minority Supplier Development Council
- National Women Business Owners Corporation
- National Gay & Lesbian Chamber of Commerce
- U.S. Business Leader Network
- National Association of Minority and Women-Owned Law Firms (NAMWOLF)

Supplier diversity programs require careful consideration and discussion to ensure the program will fit properly within your organization. The program should be developed as a collaborative effort between the purchasing team, the technology team, and the diversity professional. Ongoing oversight and management of the program may best lie with the individuals who have oversight of the organization's purchasing program, as a supplier diversity initiative can be very extensive.

Insight: Supplier Diversity Programs

An Interview with Sylvia James, Diversity Counsel, Baker Botts

Many corporations and some law firms have a comprehensive supplier diversity program. One of the more comprehensive programs in a law firm is the one established by Baker Botts. In this section, Sylvia James shares details on the challenges and opportunities of a supplier diversity program. James explains that there are five levels of classification in the supplier diversity arena: no program, basic, traditional, advanced, and world class. Baker Botts has an advanced program, which requires, among other things, a supplier diversity statement, CEO or senior management commitment, accountability, metrics and reporting, and a dedicated administrator.

An advanced program must also "have goals and objectives typically stated as a percentage of your total procurement that you will spend directly with diverse suppliers." Advanced supplier diversity programs generally establish both tier one and tier two goals. A first-tier program measures money spent directly with the women and diverse suppliers; a second-tier program measures money spent indirectly through vendors—for example, requiring a printer or mailroom service to allocate a specific percentage of their work to women- and minority-owned companies. "Another example of our tier-two program is that whenever we have a build-out at the firm, if our prime contractor is not a woman- or minority-owned company, we put in the contract a goal that the prime contractor spend 20 percent of their spend with women- and minority-owned companies."

Important components of a supplier diversity initiative include:

- Reasonable concrete goals and objectives: "We started out with a very modest goal of 1 percent of our total discretionary purchasing for the calendar year." James describes each office as having its own specific goals.
- Accountability: "Everyone knows what the goals are for the calendar year, those are stated on the intranet, and on a quarterly basis, I let the office administrators know their progress against the goals. At the end of the year, we report to everyone and then the partners in charge have

to explain to the executive committee if they do not reach their goals."

- Financial department support: "We have companies coded as women-owned or minority-owned and they run a report for me on a quarterly basis on how much money we've spent. Since I've been here, for eight years, the offices have all met or exceeded their goals. When it appears that an office is way over its goals each year, I will increase the goals. Our ultimate goal is to spend 10 percent of our spend with women- and minority-owned vendors—right now, we're spending roughly 6 to 7 percent.
- Training, mentoring, and education: "When we started this program, supplier diversity training classes were held in each one of our offices for managers, paralegals, and directors of administration, basically anyone who procures services on behalf of the firm. That training included the business case for the supplier diversity, how to find and work with diverse suppliers, and the rewards of doing so. We developed an electronic database to identity capable women- and minority-owned companies that have already been certified and have been registered to do business with us."
- Outreach: "Just like recruiting for female and minority legal talent, you've got to go out there and identity the qualified women- and minority-owned businesses producing the goods and services that we need."

Baker Botts uses a virtual aspect to outreach: a supplier diversity portal. The firm hosts a portal on its website where potential suppliers can register and communicate with the firm. Once their eligibility has been established, they can become part of the resource portal that is available internally to Baker Botts' procurement teams when they are looking to find diverse suppliers.

"I think the real reason why we continue to do this is that we really believe in the program and want to provide opportunities to women- and minority-owned businesses. The supplier diversity program is a source of pride for the firm and something that's just part of the firm's culture."

Questions to Ask When Considering a Supplier Diversity Program

- Do you have executive and financial support for the program and the internal structure to support it?

- Do you have the expertise to run the program (e.g., previous supplier diversity experience)?
- Do you have the support of the financial department? Do you have a coding system and databases?
- Do you know what kind of program would work best? Will it include Tier I and Tier II spend?
- Will you require certification from one of the certifying groups?

Also consider the following:

- Staff support (accounting, senior level engagement)
- Critical memberships in groups that provide access to database and information, which can cost up to $15,000 a year
- The time investment required of the diversity professional and others in the firm

POSSIBLE AREAS IN WHICH TO CONSIDER SUPPLIER DIVERSITY

- Professional recruiters who provide staffing (legal secretaries, IT staff, records retrieval, temps)
- Commercial printing
- Promotional items, external executive gifts
- Public relations
- Facilities, fixtures, and equipment
- Coffee and beverage services; cleaning services

What You Should Know

- Be sure you are prepared to embark upon this kind of program. You should review your resources and the internal allies who will actively support this effort.
- Be prepared to use a lot of metrics to communicate the efficacy of this effort.
- Verify your proposed budget as there will be external costs of engaging and participating in organizations that assist in certification

CHAPTER 17

SOCIAL MEDIA MEETS DIVERSITY

Or should we or shouldn't we?

Overview

Social media is a real-time and ever-changing medium and can serve as an efficient and innovative vehicle to inform, promote, persuade, and advance your diversity and inclusion efforts and brand. The decision to engage in and develop a social media platform should be made carefully and in partnership with your media and marketing professionals. In addition to sufficient content to support the social media avenues you have selected, it is important to identify and appreciate the amount of internal resources needed to keep the accounts you have created continuously updated with new information and data.

Getting Started

The diversity professional in partnership with the organization's communications professionals should start by developing a strategic social media plan, setting forth goals and objectives that are consistent with the organization's overall social media policy and strategy. Plan objectives may include direct outreach to a specific demographic for purposes of delivering information, notices, and event invitations. Identify your intended audiences, the social media platform(s) that you would like to use, and the process for identifying and approving desired content. The platform used will impact the resources, content, and planning required to keep it robust and relevant. For example, the expected amount of content needed for a Twitter site or Instagram may be very different than that needed for a Facebook or LinkedIn page. Depending on your social media policy, you may be required to use existing systems for approving content, or you may need to put in place a system to review and approve content before it is posted on your social media sites.

Next, determine if you will utilize (i.e., add content to) the organization's existing social media sites, such as Facebook, LinkedIn, and Twitter, or if you will develop separate sites focused on the organization's diversity efforts. The creation of new sites will require additional planning, as well as a detailed implementation plan and time table. Taking advantage of social media education programs, including instruction on how to use the different types of platforms, can be helpful and is encouraged. Even if a person is experienced in social media use for individual purposes, he or she may not be aware of other capabilities and resources that are available for business use. Collaborating with your organization's technology department is also important in developing your strategy and managing your social media initiative.

A critical consideration of incorporating a social media platform into your diversity and inclusion efforts is a commitment to be consistent in the delivery of content and an appreciation of the time and effort needed to identify, approve, and post content. Content is key to the success of the site, and the diversity professional should identify who will be responsible for content writing and posting early in the process. Consider if you will use original content, which is often most desirable, although arguably the most time-intensive. Original content may be in the form of blogs or other types of discussions that can be interactive and invite thought discussion and feedback. Alternatively, content may be limited to informational use only, such as a calendar of events. There is also an array of other possibilities, such as program listings, identified resources, articles, and other information. Content may also focus on your organization's efforts in a particular area, for example highlighting your organization's efforts in the area of community service, sharing quick updates for recruiting purposes, or broadly covering global diversity and inclusion efforts focused in many geographical areas.

Although multiple people may contribute to your social media content, consider the impact of maintaining a consistent voice for posting content. If not already a part of your organization's social media policy, consider developing criteria for content and posting protocols. Further, identifying sufficient content prior to the implementation of the site is encouraged and will assist in content planning. It is not helpful to have a site up and ready to go, and then have to scramble to identify content to populate the site.

Ongoing Commitment

Social media sites that are not properly cared for or that are populated with outdated content and fail to educate the reader serve little purpose, and in fact may have a negative impact on your overall diversity and inclusion goals. It is important to appreciate the objectives of any investment in social media and assess the resources available to execute your strategy. Social media is a two-way street. It can be an effective means for communicating as well as receiving information. It also can be a perilous road where one must be mindful of security issues, including access by nonapproved users, as well as sensitive content, and the impact on the organization's cyber footprint and data privacy concerns. Security policies and protocols are an important aspect in developing a social media platform. In exploring social media, consider the following:

- Why is social media relevant to your efforts?
- Who will oversee this effort once it is established? Will it be the responsibility of the diversity professional, or the social media/marketing team?
- What is the company and/or firm's policy on social media? Will additional policies or protocols be needed?
- What purpose will this initiative serve? What needs will it meet?
- What costs, if any, are involved?
- Is there a realistic expectation of the work involved?
- Are there resources available to manage the process?
- What are the short-term and long-term goals? Is there a timetable for the short-term goals?
- Is there a targeted audience with a specific purpose?
- Will the intended use of the site be limited to certain programs, such as recruiting efforts?

- Who will develop the content? How will the content be delivered?
- How will the content be maintained and updated?
- Are there any data privacy concerns in connection with site content?
- What metrics will be employed to measure the desired objectives and goals?
- Is this effort worth the output? With limited resources, is this the best use of your time and resources?

Engaging in social media is an exciting and creative initiative. Careful planning is critical in managing the process. Once established, social media may be seamlessly integrated into your organization's diversity and inclusion plan. Keep in mind that this medium is not static and will require ongoing strategy and thought to maintain your desired outreach and impact goals.

Annual reviews and updates of your social media goals and objectives with input from your organization's marketing or communications team is essential.

What You Should Know

- Do not start down this road unless you are prepared to stay on it and go where it takes you.
- Be sure to have experts around you.
- Have a plan for consistency and delivery of content.
- Do not become too attached to any ideas or mediums. Go with where you find success with your goals.
- Different mediums have different audiences. Know the difference.
- Stay on top of the metrics of success. Pay attention and evaluate whether it is worth the investment.

CHAPTER 18

DIVERSITY FATIGUE

Or this is very serious

Overview

Advancing diversity and inclusion goals in an organization requires organizational change. The diversity professional leading or charged with this effort, either in a senior or supporting capacity, is a change agent for the organization. Serving as a change agent is exciting and incredibly rewarding work; however, it is not surprising that this work can be emotionally grueling and exhausting, given the repetitive nature of the work, anticipated and recurring resistance, and the time and patience required to realize set goals and appreciate measurable differences.

Diversity fatigue is slow-moving and a common side effect of this work, and not always readily recognizable. Following is a list of signs that may indicate the onset of diversity fatigue. Although you may not experience all, it is helpful to identify the signs and recognize the need to address them.

- Exhaustion from finding different ways to say the same thing so that it is understood, is palatable, is politically correct, is not professional suicide, and still has some reasonable relationship to what you actually mean.
- A sense of defeat when things go very wrong, exactly the way you predicted it weeks ago, and everyone is looking at you to fix it, without acknowledging that it was ever discussed.
- Weariness from wearing the mask, the consistent smile, the ever-present diplomacy, the willingness to see things their way. Always

feeling like you want to stand on a desk, get everyone's attention, and say, "Hey, here is the truth, straight with no chaser!"

- Tiredness from always engaging the powerful nonbelievers, and maybe the not-so-powerful, whose resistance you must manage with a smile and diplomacy, while trying to oversimplify it, or prove it up.
- The frustration of feeling that maybe you are the only one who cares and wondering if you can really do it by yourself.
- The difficulty of having too few times when you can be authentic and use your authentic voice.
- Feeling that "There is too much work to do and I cannot get it all done *ever*!"
- The pressure from too many demands, too many masters, too many clients, too many voices in your head, too much with too little all by yourself.
- Feeling hopeless and helpless, with not enough fruitful experiences.
- Wondering how you keep going when you are never (or rarely) thanked, appreciated, or emotionally rewarded with an "Atta girl!" or "Atta guy!"

The plan for addressing diversity fatigue is individual, but you may start by asking the following questions:

- What can you do when you feel you just have too much work to do?
- How do you find a way to manage that gives you a sense of accomplishment?
- How do you cope when you cannot find your authentic voice? What do you do when you feel you are not being heard and people make the same mistakes after your advice and counsel?
- How can you manage the times when you really question whether you have lost your mind and you think, "This diversity stuff doesn't look like it will ever work"?
- How do you find the energy to stay pleasant, optimistic, and encouraging?
- How do you continue to be a believer? How do you convince others to continue believing?
- How do you find ways to be more effective and thus reduce your stress levels?

- What should you do when you feel you are alone?
- How do you spot diversity fatigue in your leaders, colleagues, advocates, and the underrepresented attorneys and staff for whom you are doing this work?
- How do you encourage them, particularly when you need encouragement yourself or you feel that it's a lost cause?
- What do you do when the attorneys at your firm who have been strong advocates, supporters, and workers get discouraged and want to give up the cause because they do not believe that the organization values their contributions to diversity, they do not believe that the organization rewards their efforts, and they feel tired from giving so much for so little return?

Explore the answers to these questions with colleagues in the diversity field. Organizations such as the Association of Law Firm Diversity Professionals, Leadership Council for Legal Diversity, Minority Corporate Council Association, Corporate Women of Color, affinity bar associations and others offer communities of support.

As easy as it sounds, when being a change agent feels like it is overwhelming, it is OK to take a break. Take deep breaths. Think of your successes. Remind yourself why you took the position in the first place. Remember why you are committed. You care. You can and you will try to do your best. Breathe.

What You Should Know

- You are not alone. Everyone in this work experiences diversity fatigue. Find a buddy who lets you vent.
- Sometimes diversity fatigue is interpreted as institutional weariness of diversity or political correctness. Know how this expression is being used and respond accordingly. If it is institutional diversity fatigue, listen, appreciate, and try to understand. Then continue to engage, communicate, and educate.

CHAPTER 19

CONCLUSION

As a diversity professional within a law firm or other organization, you are charged with developing and implementing a program to create a more diverse and inclusive workforce in a manner that is consistent with the organization's business goals and culture. This is an enormously challenging responsibility. Executed well, it is also very rewarding. Ultimately, you're trying to change the behavior of the organization as a whole and the mindset of individuals within the organization. To accomplish those goals, you need to develop a fully thought out and comprehensive strategic plan and implement the plan in a consistent manner. In so doing, you will help to make diversity an enduring part of the firm's culture.

Of course, you can lead the charge, but you can't do it alone. You need a buy-in from a host of stakeholders. Developing lines of communication and establishing trust with key players within the firm is essential. For diversity and inclusion initiatives to be successful, the organization's leaders must value the benefits and goals of diversity in the same way they value other important business issues. Leaders must voice the commitment of the senior management team to all lawyers, principals, and stakeholders in the organization. The delivery must be clear and concise, reinforcing that diversity is important and necessary and must be valued by everyone in the organization. In developing and implementing a strategic plan, the diversity professional also must provide firm leaders with the information they need to reinforce the message throughout the organization. Providing consistent, clear and concise communication with respect to your organization's diversity and inclusion strategies and programs is essential. As a diversity professional, you need to constantly inform, educate, promote, and persuade.

As discussed in Chapter 7, diversity recruiting and retention are often the hallmark of diversity programs. Indeed, effective recruiting is usually the best means for achieving short- and long-term diversity and inclusion goals, as it is essential to first build a diverse workforce. Every aspect of diversity recruiting should be strategic. The diversity professional must work hand in hand with the recruiting professionals and hiring committee or team to develop and implement a strategic plan that ensures diversity goals are met. You must remain vigilant in advancing the business case for implementing a diversity recruiting strategy and linking it with your organization's overall business objectives and goals. Retention is no less important than recruiting. In the final analysis, retention is the essence of success for the organization and answers the question of whether you are successfully recruiting and developing your human capital. A comprehensive and thoughtful infrastructure and framework must be in place to support the retention and advancement of all attorneys, in particular those who fall under the diversity umbrella.

The goals of the organization's diversity and inclusion efforts should be interwoven with every aspect of the organization. The diversity professional must interact with all departments, committees, and teams on a regular basis. Some of the obvious strategic relationships include professional development, associate evaluations, compensation, marketing and communications, information technology, human resources and finance. If your organization is global, you may be called upon to develop a global diversity and inclusion strategy that is aligned with the business objectives of the organization, but also accommodates the individual diversity needs of each office and jurisdiction of your organization, as discussed in Chapter 15. As a best practice and matter of good policy, your overall diversity and inclusion mission should be consistent throughout the organization; however, the individual objectives, tactical strategy, and planning needed to accomplish the stated goals should be customized and relevant to each region of your business. While the diversity focus will certainly vary in each jurisdiction, the issue of gender diversity and equality is a common theme present in almost all jurisdictions and geographic regions and is worth exploring as a starting point.

The diversity professional may also be tasked with creating and implementing a supplier diversity program with outside vendors. As discussed in Chapter 16, supplier diversity program is a business procurement program for goods and services utilizing businesses and enterprises that are at least 51 percent owned, operated, or controlled by underrepresented members of the business community, such as ethnic minorities, women, LGBT persons, veterans, or persons with disabilities. Supplier diversity programs can be an integral part of an organization's diversity and inclusion initiative.

Finally, as a diversity professional, you are expected to provide data and analytics that measure the diversity of your firm and the quantifiable impact of your diversity initiatives over time. Data will give you both past and present-day snapshots of your organization. It is an important tool in making projections and has a critical role in the diversity development of an organization.

In the quest to mold a more diverse firm, it is easy to get lost and misunderstand the paths to success, or even more basically, the very definitions of success. We hope this book provides diversity professionals with a broader sense of what is possible and a roadmap for integrating a diversity mindset into an organization's culture in order to build a more diverse and inclusive workplace and serve as an effective change agent within your organization.

INDEX